Bibliografische Information der Deutschen Nationalbibliothek:

Die Deutsche Nationalbibliothek verzeichnet diese Publikation in der Deutschen Nationalbibliografie; detaillierte bibliografische Daten sind im Internet über http://dnb.d-nb.de abrufbar.

Impressum:

Copyright © 2013 ScienceFactory

Ein Imprint der GRIN Verlags GmbH

Druck und Bindung: Books on Demand GmbH, Norderstedt, Germany

Die Ahnen von Sherlock Holmes

Edgar Allan Poe und die Anfänge der Detektivliteratur

Eva Deinzer (2009): Poe's Tales of Ratiocination - A Closer Look

Introduction

Edgar Allan Poe is considered a literary genius that did not only concentrate on one genre but also succeeded in many different types of literature. He gained a reputation as a poet, a literary critic, and as a writer of gothic tales of terror and science fiction. Through his tales of ratiocination – how he himself called them – he also became one of the first authors of crime fiction.

In this paper I intend to analyze two of his detective stories: *The Murders in the Rue Morgue* and *The Purloined Letter*. The focus will be on an analysis concerning the ratiocination – the way of deductive and inductive reasoning – performed by Dupin, the protagonist detective. Furthermore, I would like to present the question of whether Dupin really arrives at his conclusions by mere ratiocination and the process of reasoning or whether there are other things involved.

Before I delve into this problem though, I would like to present a short history of the crime story with Poe as the "inventor" of the detective story in the center. After that follows a short description and demonstration of the characteristics of Poe's detective stories as well as a characterization of the protagonist, detective Dupin. Before I conclude the paper, I will compare the Dupin stories to modern detective fiction that can be found in television programming.

Poe and the detective story

When you turn on television and browse through the channels you will find at least some programs that deal with crime and detection: from *Columbo*, to *Monk* or to the relatively new *CSI* series. Crime is as old as humanity. There has always been an interest in it. Therefore it is not surprising that crime fiction has become what it is today: A commodity good which attracts many people from different ranges of society. During the last three to four decades, crime fiction has even found its way into the academia and is no longer something that people read only for pleasure (Priestman 1). One question critics have always asked about is the beginnings of the crime story. Many claim that Edgar Allan Poe was the father of the detective story, however, let us take a brief look at the history of crime fiction before we agree with that.

Stories[1] of crime can also be found in the Old Testament, more precisely in the Book of Daniel: *Susanne and the Elders* and *Daniel and the Priest of Bel* are examples for that. And of course, the tale about Adam and Eve's oldest children: Cain who murdered his brother Abel out of jealousy. In Greek Mythology there is the story about Oedpius who unknowingly killed his father and married his mother. In the eighteenth century the cautionary tale developed: Society should be deterred from doing evil by reading about criminals and their doom. An example for this is the *Newgate Calendar* (1773) which is a collection of tales about how the prisoners of the Newgate Prison were captured, tried, and punished. A few years later William Godwin wrote his well-known novel *Caleb Williams* (1794) which is considered "as one of the most significant precursors

---

[1] The following information is from John Scaggs's *Crime Fiction* (7-32) unless otherwise indicated.

to the detective novel" (Scaggs 14). Caleb Williams (as a kind of detective) has to figure out that his aristocratic employer, Falkland, is the murderer of the local squire, Tyrrel.

The founding and the establishment of the police organizations in Europe and the USA led to the full development of the classic detective story. In France it happened as early as 1812 with the founding of the *Sûreté,* the civil police force founded by Eugène François Vidocq. With the Metropolitan Police Act of 1828, a permanent police force also was introduced in England under Sir Robert Peel. It was a response to rising crime rates in the late eighteenth and early nineteenth century due to the shifting distribution of population, the Industrial Revolution, and a large-scale unemployment. Scaggs concludes: "The inevitable response to the widespread emergence of the professional criminal was the birth of the modern policeman" (18).

In 1842, the Metropolitan Police created the 'Detective Department' and only one year before, Poe published the first of three detective stories *The Murders in the Rue Morgue* (Kayman 44). Dupin, the fictional detective in Poe's stories, is not working with the police; he is even a kind of a counterpart in that he does not hesitate to criticize them overtly:

> The Parisian police, so much extolled for acumen, are cunning, but no more. There is no method in their proceedings, beyond the method of the moment. They make a vast parade of measures; but, not unfrequently, these are so ill adapted to the objects proposed, as to put us in mind of Monsieur Jourdain's calling for his robe-de-chambre --pour mieux entendre la musique. The results attained by them are not unfrequently surprising, but, for the most part, are brought about by simple diligence and activity. When these qualities are unavailing, their schemes fail, [...] (Poe, "Murders" 152)

Alongside the introduction of the detective as a protagonist (Kayman 41) , Poe invented many motifs still in use in these kinds of stories like "the murder in the locked room, the unjustly accused suspect, analysis by psychological deduction, and the complementary solutions of the least likely person and the most likely place" (Van Leer 65). He has been imitated by a multitude of authors and screenplay writers ever since. The most famous example of this is probably the fictional detective Sherlock Holmes who was introduced by Arthur Conan Doyle in 1887 with his first detective mystery novel, *A Study in Scarlet*. Many other detective novels and short stories followed which made Doyle and his protagonist Holmes an international success.

For other authors the detective story introduced by Poe and refined by Doyle served as a kind of template. During the Golden Age (interwar period) in Great Britain, writers like Agatha Christie and Dorothy L. Sayers published many novels and stories featuring one protagonist detective: Christie's Hercule Poirot and Miss Marple and Sayers's Lord Peter Wimsey solved many mysteries in the classic 'whodunnit' style. During the same time, hardboiled private-eye fiction developed in the US with authors like Dashiell Hammett and Raymond Chandler. The stories concentrate on the character of the detective and the plot contains much violence and betrayal. In the last decades, the hard-boiled genre expanded and now also features women, ethnic minorities, and homosexuals as detectives. Another kind of crime fiction, which is often influenced by hard-boiled fiction, emerged and is now represented in literature and film: The police procedural where a team of professional police officers examine the crime together, often using advanced technology and scientific methods to find the criminal.

From this point of view it is easy to agree that Dupin in Poe's stories was the precursor of the classic detective in crime fiction. Although of course altered and adapted in many ways, the basic principle of an intelligent sleuth who usually is smarter than the police or the readership is still used in the same way. Are there any other characteristics in modern fictional detectives that have survived? To answer this question we first should look at the detective Dupin

11

and his methods of investigating.

Characteristics of Poe's Dupin stories

After having heard much about the history of the detective story, I suggest taking a closer look at the stories themselves, especially at the detective Dupin. At first I want to talk about some general characteristics that unite all three narratives, then I am giving a brief overview about the three stories, and finally I am providing a characterization of the protagonist Dupin.

It is very important that the reader differentiates between the author Poe and the protagonist Dupin. This distinction has not always been made by literary critics. The author is the one who creates the mystery of the whole story. Thoms (133) suggests that each of the Dupin stories is constructed by three 'narrators'. The narrator itself who provides the narrative frame; the criminal, who tries to obstruct the "formation of a rounded narrative" by *writing* the secret story (the crime); and Dupin as detective who in the end takes over the original narrative from the narrator by explaining how he came to the solution. The image of reading and writing the story is an analogy to the detection of the crime: The detective, as mentioned above, becomes the reader of the crime and simultaneously the author of the story since it is he who reveals the hidden story of the crime at the end. Dupin's reading of the crime is literally evident when he tries to get clues from reading newspaper articles ("Mystery" and "Murders") or when he reads the crime scene ("Murders") or when he scans the minister's office for the letter ("Letter"). With this "skilled act of reading and writing" the detective becomes the "hero" because he "uncovers what happened" (Thoms 135). In this way Dupin gains control of the (crime) story, which lifts him in a position of power over the criminal but also over the narrator (Thoms 133-141).

The reader (you and me) becomes a detective himself because he is "pushe[d] [...] away from the proffered answers and towards a renewed investigation of mystery" (Thoms 133).The reader is invited to read the secret story of the crime himself, to follow the detective, and to try to read the same as he does (Thoms 133). This invitation, however, is not supported by Dupin at all. He usually does not share his thoughts and clues till the very end of the story when he reveals what happened. The reader therefore is not able to "solve the mystery along with Dupin" (Van Leer 66).

Another characteristic of all three stories is that the plot itself does not seem to be relevant to the story. In all three narratives "the manner of [...] discovery and interpretation, and general philosophical discussions" (Van Leer 67) are placed in the center of the story. Van Leer blames this on the fractured chronology which is typical for all three tales.

Content of the stories

All Dupin stories are set in France, after the establishment of the professional police, which was a necessary condition for these tales of detective fiction. The boundaries between fact and fiction are often a little blurred in Poe's works. The same can be found here: It lies in the nature of a detective story that it pretends to deal with facts instead of fiction – in fact, some people do not even know that Sherlock Holmes was not a real detective. Especially considering the fact that Poe wrote the first stories of this kind and the readership had never seen anything like this before. In his first Sherlock Holmes adventure *A Study in Scarlet* (1887) Doyle presents the detective Holmes who "compares himself to Dupin and Lecoq, treating them as really existing historical figures" (Kayman 42).

Poe even once worked a real crime case into one of his stories, namely in the narrative with the title *The Mystery of Marie Roget* (1842). He based it on a real crime committed in New York in 1841 in which the body of a woman, Mary Rogers, was found murdered in the Hudson River. Poe transferred the story to France, altered the name of the victim, and offered a fictional solution to the case (the real case had not been solved at the time the story was published). Since this story will not be part of the following analysis, I will not go into detail concerning the content.

In his first tale of ratiocination *The Murders of the Rue Morgue* (1841) Dupin solves the case of a murder of two women which turned out to not be a murder at all. The culprit was an orangutan who was captured by a sailor and brought to France to make money. Dupin read the newspaper articles about the crime and visited the crime scene. Having established that the murder could not have been committed by a human being, but rather by an orangutan, he tricked the sailor into coming to his place and forced him to explain how everything happened.

The third and last in the series is *The Purloined Letter* (1845) in which it is clear from the beginning who committed the crime. The minister D--- stole a compromising letter from the royal apartments and is now blackmailing an unnamed lady. The police already searched his apartment but failed to obtain the letter. The prefect of the police asks Dupin to help him solve the case and Dupin uses his method of ratiocination to find the letter. Later he exchanges it with a fake one and leaves the prefect puzzled.

Dupin the detective

How is Dupin the detective? Can some of his traits still be observed in fictional detectives that surround us in modern times? A close look at the protagonist of all three stories should help answer those questions.

The narrator of the stories describes Dupin as an eccentric person when he tells the reader about his lifestyle. He is sort of a dandy figure who is definitely the opposite of an ordinary member of society. For example, he prefers sleeping during the day and going out at night. The narrator finances this lifestyle by paying for all the mutual expenses since his friend, Dupin, is without money. They met in a library and Dupin impresses with his erudition and leaves the narrator in admiration, which might be the reason for his generosity towards the detective (Poe, "Murders" 143-144). Furthermore, as a book lover, Dupin is more interested in intellectual things than abiding by social orders, and he also likes to show off his intellectual abilities (Kayman 45). He does not, however, only want to brag about it, but also he wishes to show the narrator (and the reader) that he really knows how the human mind works, and that he can draw conclusions when no one else can. In *The Murders of the Rue Morgue* he explains to the narrator at length how he was able to 'read' his thoughts (146-147).

With the introduction of the first person narrator as Dupin's friend and companion, Poe invented the typical *Watson-figure*. Almost every good fictional detective has his assistant who tells the story to an audience. In Poe's Dupin stories, the narrator remains unnamed and is the link between the detective and the reader. He acts like a foil to Dupin in regard to his mental and analytic abilities. Dupin definitely is too brilliant for the readership to identify with him, but his companion is portrayed as a little slow on the uptake and not at all ingenious. The average reader is glad to be at least a little brighter than he is. When Dupin surprises him with knowing whom he was thinking about, the narrator exclaims: "[…] this is beyond my comprehension. I do not hesitate to say that I am amazed, and can scarcely credit my senses" (Poe, "Murders" 145). Dupin often keeps him in the dark about his ongoing investigation only to reveal the whole solution at the end. In doing so, "Dupin emphasizes his superiority, creating a significant gap between his composure and control and the vulnerability of [...] his companion[...]" (Thoms 144).

Not only does his companion act like a foil, but also the police do as well. Dupin does not work with the police and consequently does not inform them about his results of the investigation either. For him, detection is like a private game. He even ridicules the police, as aforementioned (part 2). The police are only able to solve a crime if everything is in the usual order, because they are not able to dive into the criminal's mind (Poe, "Letter" 216). Dupin, on the other hand, is a brilliant detective and is the only person able to solve the cases. Scaggs sums up:

> The Paris setting contributes to the formula that Poe's stories set out by employing existing police and detective forces as a foil to Monsieur C. Auguste Dupin's analytical genius. The formulaic device, which simultaneously identifies the dull and lacklusre mental faculties of thepolice force as a whole and the brilliance of the private detective as an individual, is further emphasised (sic!) in 'The Purloined Letter' (19).

Dupin is an ambiguous character regarding his motives: In the beginning he seems objective, but later the reader recognizes that he is guided by personal reasons, or as Thoms puts it:

> [...] Dupin emerges as a worldly detective who is driven by a variety of motives: to repay 'a service' performed by le Bon; to exact personal revenge on Minister D--- for 'an evil turn'; to pursue his 'political prepossessions' by acting 'as a partisan of the lady' in the same story (137)

Ambiguity also is evident when it comes to the ostensible opposition with the criminal. It is no real opposition for a number of reasons. In the first place, he does not care about social order as I mentioned above (life style). Secondly, he enjoys having power over others. In *The Purloined Letter*, for example, he hides the letter for weeks before telling the prefect that he is in its possession and therefore accepts that the minister still can blackmail the lady (Poe, "Letter" 213-214). Another example of that can be found in *The Murders of the Rue Morgue* when Dupin is threatening the sailor:

'You shall give me all the information in your power about these murders in the Rue Morgue.' Dupin said the last words in a very low tone, and very quietly. Just as quietly, too, he walked toward the door, locked it, and put the key in his pocket. He then drew a pistol from his bosom and placed it, without the least flurry, upon the table (p. 164-165).

Here it is obvious that he does not shrink from using criminal methods himself. Apart from threatening the sailor with a gun he does not care about the sailor's moral crimes when he captures the orangutan and takes it to France. Thoms asserts that "[b]y obscuring the sailor's mistreatment of the orangutan [...] Dupin obscures his own oppressive use of power" (139). It is therefore not far-fetched that the protagonist's name – at least if you pronounce it English, not French – might be a telling name derived from the verb *to dupe* which changes to *duping*, meaning "to trick or cheat somebody"[2] (Fisher 59 and Nygaard 224). Another hint for all this is his initials: C.A.D. – cad, meaning "a man who behaves in a dishonest or unfair way"[3] (Nygaard 224). Dupin's tendency to ambiguity makes him definitely a more interesting character and he somehow is a good reflection of society itself. On the one hand, we all want to do good deeds but sometimes we just use evil methods.

Maybe because of all that, he does not have any problems diving into the mind of the criminal, taking his perspective and thinking like him. He wants to be challenged by a criminal who is kind of a mastermind like he himself is. In *The Purloined Letter* he faces an equal opponent, the minister D---, with his "daring, dashing, and discriminating ingenuity" (220). The kind of analysis and logical thinking he undertakes is called ratiocination and will be discussed more precisely in the chapter "Ratiocination and the Power of Detection".

---

[2] Definition from the OALD, 6th ed., 2000

[3] Definition from the OALD, 6th ed., 2000

Poe, with his detective Dupin, definitely introduced some character traits that were repeated in other fictional detectives as well. The eccentricity and ratiocination, for example, is also found in Sherlock Holmes and Mr. Monk, the protagonist of the televison series *Monk*. Also the *Watson-figure* is clearly something that other writers have adopted, Doyle as well as Sayers, among others. The position outside the police as a private investigator, being brighter than them, is definitely repeated in the Sherlock Holmes stories, but also in more recent detective fiction like the police procedurals where it is not the police, but rather a psychological profiler that solves the case (e.g. *The Mermaids Singing* by Val McDermid).

Ratiocination and the Power of Detection

Poe called his stories featuring Dupin as the investigator *Tales of Ratiocination*; he did not yet call them detective stories. Ratiocination is "the process of thinking or arguing about something in a logical way"[4], in short: reasoning. Reason is indeed a keyword when it comes to Dupin's method of solving crimes. He *reads* facts, brings them together and comes to a conclusion through deductive and inductive reasoning. He usually does this by reconstructing the deed: he begins at the end (the committed crime) and analyzes his way through to the beginning. He is like a "hunter for clues" which serve as "individual pieces of a larger puzzle" (Sova 122). As I have already mentioned in the chapter "Dupin the detective", Dupin is able to dive into the criminal's mind and put himself in the criminal's position. In this way he is able to solve the crimes that were believed to be insoluble.

It is not the mystery that is the focus of these stories but the analysis and method of detection that is used to solve it. Dupin possesses the analytic ability that is necessary for a successful unraveling of the crime. He observes closely and then reasons, through a series of mental steps, what happened (Sova 122). The detective – as much as Holmes later – does not really seem to be very active while solving the crime. For example, in *Murders in the Rue Morgue* he basically draws all information out of the newspaper and visits the crime scene just once. He basically solves the case from home. This kind of investigating a crime came to be known as *armchair detection* and it underlines the brilliance of

---

[4] Definition from the OALD, 6th ed., 2000

the detective even more, since he is coming to the right solution just through mental ability.

Ratiocination, though, is not possible without using imagination. If you just count the facts and concentrate on what you see, you will not be successful. Indeed, you are likely to "lose sight of the bigger picture" (Sova 153) if you focus too much on little details. In *The Purloined Letter* he demonstrates this by looking for the most obvious - a letter which is not hidden at all - instead of searching the room for hidden places with the latest scientific methods like the police did. Intuitive perception is necessary to apply ratiocination effectively. The introduction to *The Murders in the Rue Morgue* emphasizes this: "It will be found, in fact, that the ingenious are always fanciful, and the *truly* imaginative never otherwise than analytic" (142).

In the following I will demonstrate Dupin's ratiocination in *The Murders in the Rue Morgue* and *The Purloined Letter* and later examine whether Dupin really finds the truth through mere reasoning or whether there is something else which is worth mentioning.

Ratiocination in *The Murders in the Rue Morgue*

There are many examples of ratiocination in this story, but due to the limits of this paper I am only providing a few of them. The story is divided into two parts: the introduction in which the narrator explains the difference between true analysis and simple ingenuity and the plot itself.

The reader learns in the introduction that calculation is not the same as analyzing because analyzing always is in need of intuition: "His results, brought about by the very soul and essence of method, have, in truth, the whole air of intuition" (141). On the next page the narrator explains why it is the analyst that is more likely to win at a game of checkers than somebody who does not possess such abilities:

> Deprived of ordinary resources, the analyst throws himself into the spirit of his opponent, identifies himself therewith, and not unfrequently sees thus, at a glance, the sole methods (sometimes indeed absurdly simple ones) by which he may seduce into error or hurry into miscalculation (142).

Mere calculation is not helpful when it comes to analyzing a situation correctly and drawing the right conclusions. Using the analogy of playing a game of Whist, the narrator tells us that it is not the procedure "by 'the book'" (142) which takes you one step before your opponents, but the "quality of observation" (142).

In the plot itself the reader first faces Dupin's analytic abilities when he explains in detail how he came to read his friend's thoughts (142-143). Since it is quite a long monologue, I will not quote it here at length but rather in short excerpts. Dupin astonished the narrator because he knew that he was thinking about a certain man called Chantilly. He said that he "was not particularly attentive to what you did; but observation has become with me, of late, a species of necessity" (142). When his friend, the narrator, murmured the word 'sterotomy' he "knew that [he] could not say to [him]self 'stereotomy' without being brought to think of atomies, and thus of the theories of Epicurus" (142). Another example of how well the detective is able to observe and conclude is given when the narrator "draw[s] [him]self up to [his] full height" because Dupin "was sure that [he] reflected upon the diminutive figure of Chantilly" (142).

After reading about the murder case in the newspaper, Dupin is sharing his thoughts about the police work that has been done so far and the qualities of the police in general. About Vidocq he says: "He impaired his vision by holding the object too close. [...] he lost sight of the matter as a whole" (142-43). Dupin is convinced that if you look for the answers too meticulously you will not see them at all: "Truth is not always in a well. In fact, […] I do believe that she is always invariably superficial" (143). Dupin and his friend decide to go to the scene of crime to take a closer look. In the end, it is only Dupin who looks closer since the narrator does not see any necessity for this: "Dupin, meanwhile, examining the whole neighborhood, as well as the house, with a minuteness of attention for which I could see no possible object" (143). Not only do we recognize here that the detective is a very close observer, but also that he does not tell neither the narrator nor the reader what he sees and if something strikes him as unusual. He keeps us in the dark about his thoughts and therefore it is even more surprising to us and the narrator when he suddenly says "[T]he facility with which I shall arrive, or have arrived, at the solution of this mystery, is in the direct ratio of its apparent insolubility in the eyes of the police" (154).

In another very long monologue, he is explaining to us how he came to find the solution: "I proceeded to think thus – *a posteriori*" (157). He uses the method of inductive reasoning because he knows that the murderers escaped from one of the windows; and the question that is still to be answered is 'how' they did it. He elaborates his reconstruction of the case in detail (157-164) leaving the narrator in awe and just asking him some questions for which he already has the answers. Dupin stresses also the importance of probability when he talks about how the police interpret a mere coincident as a possible motive: "Coincidences, in general, are great stumbling-blocks in the way of that class of thinkers who have been educated to know nothing about the theory of probabilities" (160).

Ratiocination in *The Purloined Letter*

Poe's third tale of ratiocination, which he considered his best one (Sova 152), is shorter than the other two, but nevertheless full of examples for his method of detection and investigation. I also will provide just some of them.

When the prefect of the police came to visit Dupin and asked for his help, the detective gave a hint as to how to look differently at the case: "'Perhaps it is the very simplicity of the thing which puts you at fault'" (209). He thinks that observing something too narrow-mindedly will lead you astray. He continues telling the prefect that he probably is looking for something more obvious (209). The prefect, though, does not even realize Dupin's effort and just goes on explaining to him what happened. At the end of the prefect's story, Dupin does not offer any advice for him and so the prefect leaves without any hope to solve the case. A month later the prefect visits Dupin and his friend again and to his and the narrator's surprise, Dupin produces the letter they have been looking for so long. Later, Dupin tells his friend what his thoughts were about this case and what he did after the prefect left their house a month ago.

First, he analyzes why the prefect and the police were not able to solve this case:

> 'The measures, then,' he continued, 'were good in their kind, and well executed; their defect lay in their being inapplicable to the case and to the man. A certain set of highly ingenious resources are, with the Prefect, a sort of Procrustean bed, to which he forcibly adapts his designs' (215).

He goes on and explains to the narrator what he exactly means by using an example of a children's game called 'even and odd', where one child has to guess the amount of marbles another child is hiding in his hands. He once knew a child who was really good at guessing the marbles so he asked him why he was so lucky, the child answered that "[he] fashion[ed] the expression of [his] face, as accurately as possible, in accordance with the expression of his [opponent], and then wait to see what thoughts or sentiments ar[o]se in [his] mind or heart, as if to match with the expression'" (216). The narrator concludes correctly, that "[i]t is merely an identification of the reasoner's intellect with that of his opponent"

(215). What Dupin wants to express by that little analogy is that the police are unable to think outside their usual procedure: "'They consider only their *own* ideas of ingenuity; and, in searching for any thing hidden, advert only to the modes in which *they* would have hidden it. [...] but when the cunning of the individual felon is diverse in character from their own, the felon foils them, of course'" (216). The minister D— , on the contrary, is not that ignorant but rather clever and ingenious. Dupin knows him as a mathematician and a poet, which means "he would reason well" whereas "as mere mathematician, he could not have reasoned at all, and thus would have been at the mercy of the Prefect" (217). The minister D— is an equal opponent for Dupin; he is somebody who has the same intellect and the same acumen as the detective and it is therefore very interesting for Dupin to outwit him.

Dupin demonstrates once again that it is easy to overlook the obvious if you concentrate on the tiny little details instead of looking for the bigger picture when he talks about the game of puzzles which is typically played on a map. One group is supposed to find the name of a street or a river the other group tells them. Dupin remarks that

'a novice in the game generally seeks to embarrass his opponents by giving them the most minutely lettered names; but the adept selects such words as stretch, in large characters, from one end of the chart to the other. These [...] escape observation by dint of being excessively obvious' (219).

For Dupin, it is clear that the prefect of the police "never once thought it probable, or possible, that the minister had deposited the letter immediately beneath the nose of the whole world, by way of best preventing any portion of that world from perceiving it" (219). Dupin, knowing that the police only looked for the details and the apparently hidden places, decided to go to the minister's home in person in order to look for the letter himself. And he found it: "No sooner had I glanced at this letter than I concluded it to be that of which I was in search. To be sure, it was, to all appearance, radically different from the one of which the Prefect had read us so minute a description" (220). This obvious difference from the original letter was what drew Dupin's attention toward it. He wasn't fooled by the apparent randomness with which this letter was displayed.

Never trust the detective's method

As we have seen above, Dupin really seems to be brilliant at his ratiocinations and his way of analyzing. He also seems to be always right with his conclusions. He seems like a man the reader can trust, because he is always in search of the truth. But is he really? As I have already mentioned in the chapter "Dupin the detective" he is also a little bit like a criminal himself. But the reader still tends to trust his conclusions. But the reader should know better: Poe is very well known for his "eccentric or half-mad narrators" and he more than once created hoaxes which the readership first believed to be true (Nygaard 223). We really should be more careful when it comes to believing Dupin and his methods or even his intentions. Let us have a closer look:

For Dupin, analysis seems often like a game. He even thinks it is an "amusement" (Poe, "Murders" 153) that distracts him from the boredom of his daily routine. This, however, means that he has to be somehow detached from what is going on. He needs a distance in order to be objective. And that is exactly how Dupin and other famous fictional detectives like Holmes or Hercule Poirot are: "loners and eccentrics, isolated individuals with little in the way of family ties or other commitments" (Nygaard 225). There is one more thing that the analogy of the games illustrates so well: Does the detective really want to find the truth or does he just want to win the game? These two aims – finding the truth and winning the game – are by no means compatible. Dupin, although he seems to find the truth, also likes winning, especially when it means succeeding over the police. He also is eager to win when he steals the letter from the minister D— and takes revenge by leaving him in the dark. Also, we know about the little rivalry between him and the narrator: Dupin always displays his mental superiority over the narrator by demonstrating his analytic abilities so well and later talking about them at length. But there is another game going on: namely the one between the "narrator and the reader, author and audience" (Nygaard 227). The narrator indeed tells us the rules of the game when he philosophizes about analysis in the beginning of *The Murders of the Rue Morgue*:

> Deprived of ordinary resources, the analyst throws himself into the spirit of his opponent, identifies himself therewith, and not infrequently sees thus, at a glance, the sole methods (sometimes indeed absurdly simple ones) by which he may seduce into error or hurry into miscalculation (142)

Loisa Nygaard sums up: "Thus the objective of the analyst is to 'seduce into error' or 'hurry into miscalculation,' to trick and deceive" (228).

How exactly does Dupin use the power of ratiocination? He applies a combination of deduction and induction (Nygaard 229). Nygaard gives explanations of these two methods:

> Deductive reasoning is generally defined to be reasoning from premises to specific conclusions according to the set rules of logic.[...]Deduction has also been called reasoning *a priori*, from first principles, and sometimes crudely characterized as reasoning from cause to effect. [...]

> Induction [...] involves reasoning from a body of evidence to more general conclusions [...]. Induction has also been referred to at times as reasoning *a posteriori*, 'from what comes after', or reasoning from effect to cause (230-231).

It is clearly this latter kind of analysis he applies most often; hints at deduction occur less frequently and when they do, "he does so primarily for strategic reasons, in order to lend a greater aura of certainty to his conclusions" (Nygaard 230). If you deduce something, it is more likely to be true than when you induce something. In other words, when you have a set of rules and you are supposed to come to conclusions from this, set you will be more likely to arrive at the correct conclusions than when you have specific examples and you have to find the general set of rules behind them. Who guarantees that there is only one possible set of rules? And how do you know if the one you found is true? Hence, the method of induction is not always reliable because we simply assume that the future will be exactly like the past (Nygaard 232). When applying inductive reasoning, Dupin assumes that everybody and everything will behave and be like he used to know it. He does not even consider that people and things might react in a different way today than they did yesterday. And I think it is clear that this might be true, but just as well might not be true. Not only is somebody who uses induction relying on the nature's habit but also they are always in danger of the discovery of new evidence: There is a possibility "that the conclusion will be contradicted by new evidence that might become available in the future" (Nygaard 234). Another fact that weakens the credibility of induction compared to deduction is that even if you find a piece of evidence which is true, then your conclusion is not automatically true as well. There might be more than one possible conclusion and nobody is able to say which one is definitely the right one.

Dupin sometimes agrees with the uncertainty of this kind of conclusion and sometimes he tries to hide the fact that they are the only possible options among many. In *The Murders of the Rue Morgue* he gives the following answer to his friend's question about how he can be sure that the sailor belongs to a Maltese vessel: "'I do *not* know it […] I am not *sure* of it. […] Now if, after all, I am wrong in my induction […] still I can have done no harm in saying what I did […]'" (163). Here he is accepting the possibility of another conclusion because it would not be such an obstacle in his way to solve the mystery. In another comment, though, he does not use the word *induction* to describe his process of reasoning but *deduction*. He clearly wants to stress that there is no other option – at least not for him – because if there were, then Dupin would not have solved the case:

> 'I do not hesitate to say that legitimate deductions even from this portion of testimony – the portion respecting the gruff and shrill voices – are in themselves sufficient to engender a suspicion which should give direction to all farther progress in the investigation of the mystery. I said 'legitimate deductions'; but my meaning is not thus fully expressed. I designed to imply that the deductions are the sole proper ones, and that the suspicion arises *inevitably* from them as the single result' (Poe, "Murders" 156).

Here it becomes obvious that Dupin is trying to deceive everybody: the narrator, the police and us, the readers, when he implies that his conclusions are "the sole proper ones". He is very good at hiding the uncertainties from the readership. He pretends to be very thorough in his thinking and the way he investigates every possibility, so that the readers finally are convinced that he really found the one and only solution to the crime (Nygaard 237). Sometimes, however, he does not really reason very well. In other words, he tends to be too superficial in his argumentation. When he explains to the narrator why he thinks that the voice the neighbors heard cannot be human, he clearly dismisses the more obvious conclusions in favor of his orangutan theory: "'You will say that it might have been the voice of an Asiatic – of an African. Neither Asiatics nor Africans abound in Paris'" (Poe, "Murders" 156). As Loisa Nygaard points ironically out: "Now as wide-awake critics have been quick to point out, orangutans do not abound in Paris" (239). She also writes in her essay that

> Poe sets up the scene and circumstances for Dupin's final explication of the mystery [in the rue Morgue] in a clever but decidedly peculiar fashion that indicates that there are numerous interpretive possibilities that Dupin has failed to consider in his drive to solve the crime and to discover the perpetrator (239).

She mentions some of them on page 240 to 242 which I do not want to reiterate in my paper but which clearly demonstrate that Poe wanted the reader to be left in doubt about the real and true solution to the mystery. The readers "are in possession of the pieces of the puzzle but still do not know the full story" (Nygaard 242).

To sum this all up we can say that if Dupin arrived at the right conclusions, if the cases really happened the way he is convinced of, then he did not manage this through the process of reasoning but simply through guessing and the right intuition, in short: because he was lucky (Nygaard 245-246). And, moreover, he knew about this: He constantly "plays down the material evidence, stressing instead his own analytical brilliance" (Nygaard 248). His ratiocinations are brilliant but nevertheless he needs intuition and luck to find the right solution, but he constantly "clothe[s] them in the forms of reasoning accepted in his day, that is, in the conventions of inductive and deductive logic" (Nygaard 248).

Dupin as a template for modern detectives

Although Poe's tales of ratiocination were the precursor for many detective stories, they are not really well known anymore. Everybody, though, remembers the many stories of Arthur Conan Doyle featuring Sherlock Holmes as the detective. We already have established that it was Poe who presented the template for this, and now I would like to show how modern detectives in television programs still can be traced back to that model.

The TV show *Monk* features Adrian Monk (Tony Shalhoub) a former detective for the San Francisco Police Department suffering from an obsessive compulsive disorder which has gotten worse since his wife was killed by a car bomb. After his wife died, he had a nervous breakdown and was discharged from the police. Now he is serving as a private detective and consultant for the police. He has a female nurse accompanying him in everyday life and at work, so that he is able to focus on the crime cases.

In *House M.D.*, the protagonist is Dr. Gregory House (Hugh Laurie), a brilliant but sarcastic and somewhat antisocial physician who together with his team of overqualified doctors and his friend Dr. James Wilson has to fight some medical battles which they usually win. He is really excellent in diagnosing ostensibly impossible cases, a fact that leads to his particular nature which is cocky and arrogant, rather than moderate and likeable. Although *House M.D.* is not a classic detective story, since there is basically no detective as such, it can be regarded as one. Dr. House solves medical cases instead of crime cases, but the way he does it can be compared to the way a detective does it: Looking for clues, talking to victims, even searching the "crime scene" (he sometimes sends his team to look for substances in the patients' houses). Stacey Gibson defines the show as follows: "[…] a hospital whodunit in which doctors sleuth their way through symptoms until they find the medical culprit".

What do Adrian Monk, Gregory House, and C. Auguste Dupin have in common? Of course, you could find more matches with and allusions to Sherlock Holmes (e.g. Gregory House's apartment number is 221B), because we simply "know" Holmes better than Dupin and Holmes had the chance to "tell" us more about himself since he was the protagonist of many novels and short stories whereas Dupin only appeared in three. Holmes, however, is not of my particular interest for this paper.

All three characters are brilliant at what they do, they are intelligent and ingenious, and they always come to the right conclusion. They all use the method of deductive and inductive reasoning, or ratiocination, by observing and drawing conclusions. Monk uses a special concentration technique with his hands every time he is on a new crime scene and has a brilliant ability to connect information that, on first glance, is totally irrelevant to the case. Dr. House usually is portrayed deep in thought when the solution finally strikes him. And Dupin also does not investigate by trial and error, as we have seen above, but through observing and putting himself in the criminal's mind.

Another similarity among the three of them is the eccentricity they all share. They all have a tendency to be rather anti-social. Dupin does not live an ordinary life; he sleeps during the day and is awake at night. Monk has this obsessive compulsive disorder which does not allow him to socialize too much with people because he usually is disgusted by them. He does not like human contact like shaking hands, uses sanitary wipes all the time to get rid of the germs, and has many phobias (milk, lady bugs, and needles, among others). Dr. House is clearly not a friendly person: Wendell Wittler described him as "[a]nti-social, misanthropic, cynical, abrasive, abusive, smug" and added that "there aren't many negative adjectives you could not use to describe him". House said in Season 1, Episode 4: "People don't bug me until they get teeth".

The assistant-friend is also something they all have in common. Dupin and the unnamed narrator live together and the narrator is kind of an assistant and friend to him. We do not learn much about this relationship though. Dr. House has one close friend, Dr. James Wilson, who also works in the clinic and is definitely also an assistant to him since he sometimes helps him solve the case. Dr. Wilson is the only one who sometimes can glimpse behind House's façade. Natalie Teeger is Mr. Monk's assistant. She helps him organizing his everyday life, hands him sanitary wipes and also is a great help solving the cases. All these assistants, though, are not as smart as the detective himself which contributes to our perception of his brilliance.

This is also true for the police which serve as a counterpart to the detective. In the Dupin stories, it is the prefect of the police in particular and the police in general who are portrayed as rather ignorant and incapable. Dr. House does not work with the police or against them, but he works with a team of doctors that are intelligent but still think in ways too straightforward and are usually wrong in the end. House does not explicitly work against them, but he does not think highly of them either. Monk often works as a private consultant for the San Francisco police, more precisely for Captain Leland Stottlemeyer and Lieutenant Randy Disher. Randy is often presented as a clumsy and sometimes dumb police officer. In the end, it is always Monk and not the police who solve the crime because they just went their usual way.

Conclusion

We have learned that we cannot trust Dupin, but nevertheless we do anyway. We are fascinated by his way of investigating as well as by the way his fictional followers investigate. We tend not to look to closely when something does not add up. We are convinced that it simply must be our fault when we do not understand something. The detective's brilliance is something we do not like to doubt. That is one reason why detective fiction has become what it is today. We do not want our image of the mastermind detective to be destroyed.

After this analysis, it suggests that Poe might have intended these stories to fool the reader once again; the way he created hoaxes several times before and after these detective stories. He deliberately constructed the stories in a way that the reader cannot really be sure about the detective's intentions and methods. Because of Dupin's character and reliability he pretends he has, we are, however, very likely to fall for him and his game. He has – or at least pretends to have – some kind of authority which is the reason why so many readers do not manage to look behind his façade.

Bibliography

Primary sources

Poe, Edgar Allan. "The Murders in the Rue Morgue". *The Complete Tales and Poems of Edgar Allan Poe.* London, et al.: Penguin, 1982, 141-168.

Poe, Edgar Allan. "The Mystery of Marie Roget.". *The Complete Tales and Poems of Edgar Allan Poe.* London, et al.: Penguin, 1982, 169-207.

Poe, Edgar Allan. "The Purloined Letter". *The Complete Tales and Poems of Edgar Allan Poe.* London, et al.: Penguin, 1982, 208-222.

Secondary sources

Fisher, Benjamin F. *The Cambridge Introduction to Edgar Allan Poe.* New York: University Press, 2008.

Kayman, Martin A. "The short story from Poe to Chesterton". *The Cambridge Companion to Crime Fiction.* Cambridge: University Press, 2006. 41-57.

Nygaard, Loisa. "Winning the Game: Inductive Reasoning in Poe's 'Murders in the Rue Morgue'". *Studies in Romanticism.*Boston: Routledge, 1994, 33:2, 223-254.

Priestman, Martin. "Introduction: crime fiction and detective fiction". *The Cambridge Companion to Crime Fiction.* Cambridge: University Press, 2006. 1-6.

Scaggs, John. *Crime Fiction.* London: Routledge, 2005.

Sova, Dawn B. *Critical Companion to Edgar Allan Poe: a literary reference to his life and work*. New York: Facts on File, 2007.

Thoms, Peter. "Poe's Dupin and the power of detection". *The Cambridge Companion to Edgar Allan Poe*. Cambridge: University Press, 2002, 133-147.

Van Leer, David. "Detecting the Truth: The World of the Dupin Tales". *New Essays on Poe's Major Tales*. Cambridge: University Press, 1993, 65-91.

Internet sources

Davis, J. Madison. "Mr. Monk and the pleasing paradigm":

http://findarticles.com/p/articles/mi_hb5270/is_3_83/ai_n31844174/

03.10.09

Wittler, Wendell. "Living in a 'House' built for one":

http://www.msnbc.msn.com/id/7518037/

03.10.09

Bernhard Kehler (2009): Geheimnis und Detektion. Edgar Allen Poes Erzählungen "The Murders in the Rue Morgue" und "The Purloined Letter" als Vorbild für ein neues Genre

Einleitung

Erläuterung und Eingrenzung des Themas

Edgar Allen Poe hat ein breites Spektrum literarischen Schaffens abgedeckt, welches sich vom Gedicht über die Kurzgeschichte bis hin zu zahlreichen Rezensionen, Kritiken und theoretisch-ästhetischen Literaturbetrachtungen erstreckt. Berühmt wurde er mit seinen so genannten „Tales of Ratiocination" und mit den „Gothic Tellings".

Diese Hausarbeit hat zum Ziel seine Detektivgeschichten „The Murders in the Rue Morgue" und „The Purloined Letter" zu untersuchen.

Zwei Fragen stehen dabei im Vordergrund, zum einen das Verfahren der Detektion zur Lösung eines Kriminalfalles und zum anderen die Konstruktion einer Detektivgeschichte als Short-Story. Für beide Aspekte erhebt Poe den Anspruch einer logischen Strenge, wie sie vornehmlich in der Mathematik vorzufinden ist.

Den ersten Aspekt, das Verfahren der Detektion, reflektiert er ausführlich innerhalb der beiden Erzählungen, während er den zweiten Aspekt, die Konstruktion einer Detektivgeschichte in seinen literaturtheoretischen Betrachtungen explizit erläutert.

Um das Wesen der „Detective Stories" auszuloten, ist es erforderlich sowohl wissenschaftstheoretische als auch poetologisch-ästhetische Überlegungen einzubeziehen um daraus das sich mit Poe etablierende Genre zu erschließen.

Grundstruktur der beiden Erzählungen

Die Komposition der Detektivgeschichten

In „The Philosophy of Composition" formuliert E.A. Poe seinen wichtigsten Grundsatz für die Komposition eines Gedichtes, der sich auch auf die Kurzgeschichte übertragen lässt:

> Nothing is more clever, than that every plot, worth the name, must be elaborated to its denouement before anything be attempted with the pen. It is only with the denouement constantly in view that we can give a plot its indispensable air of consequence, or causation, by making the incidents, and especially the tone at all points, tend to the development of the intention. [5]

Mit dieser Forderung nach kausaler Strenge betritt E.A. Poe nicht unbedingt Neuland. Schon Aristoteles konstatierte in seiner Poetik:

> Die Tragödie ist die Nachahmung einer guten in sich geschlossenen Handlung. [6]

Lessing erhob in seiner Hamburgischen Dramaturgie ergänzend den Anspruch, dass ein Genie sich nur mit Gegebenheiten beschäftigen könne, die ineinander begründet seien, sich also als Ketten von Ursache und Wirkung darstellen lassen.

Wenn E.A. Poe diesen Anspruch ebenso auf die „Short-Story" und damit auch auf seine „Detective Stories" bezieht, bewegt er sich also auf den Pfaden einer langen Tradition. Neu ist allerdings, dass Poe dem Zeitgeist folgend die kausale Strenge eines Plots aus der Mathematik abzuleiten versucht. In „The Philosophy of Composition" konstatiert er in Bezug auf das Gedicht "The Raven":

---

[5] Poe, E.A.: The Philosophy of Composition, S. 675

[6] Aristoteles: Poetik, S. 19

It is my design to render it manifest that no one point in its composition is referrible either to accident or intuition – that the work proceeded, step by step, to its completion, with the precision and rigid consequence of a mathematical problem.[7]

Historische Wurzeln für die Übertragung mathematischer Denkmuster auf die Dichtung lassen sich bis in die Goethezeit hinein zurückverfolgen. Novalis betrieb intensive mathematische Studien. Tieck dachte über den Zusammenhang von Mathematik, Musik und Farben nach und Heinrich von Kleist sah ein Ideal darin, sich gleichermaßen auf „Metapher" und „Formel" zu verstehen.[8]

Neben diesem Anspruch, den Plot einer Erzählung mit der kausalen Strenge eines Mathematikers zu konstruieren, weisen die Detektivgeschichten des Autors einige erzähltechnische Besonderheiten auf:

Alewyn weist darauf hin, dass der Kriminalroman die Geschichte eines Verbrechens erzählt, während der Detektivroman die Aufdeckung desselben schildert. Des Weiteren stellt er fest, dass in einem Kriminalroman die Erzählung parallel zum Geschehen verläuft, während in einer Detektivgeschichte das Pferd quasi von hinten aufgezäumt wird. Der finale Punkt des Kriminalromans, in der Regel ein Mord, wird dabei zum Ausgangspunkt des Detektivromans. Der Rest der Erzählung beschäftigt sich mit der Rekonstruktion des Verbrechens und seinen Wurzeln. Die eine Form des Erzählens kann man als progressiv bezeichnen, die andere als invertiert oder rückläufig. Als Beispiel für die erste Erzählform führt Alewyn die biblische Erzählung der Ermordung Abels durch Kain an. Dort verläuft die Erzählung parallel zum Geschehen. Als Prototyp für die zweite Erzählform verweist er auf

---

[7] Poe, E.A.: (wie Anm.1), S. 676-677

[8] Kreuzer, Helmut: Mathematik und Dichtung, S.9

das Enthüllungsdrama des König Ödipus. In dieser Tragödie wird erstmals ein Verbrechen analytisch rekonstruiert.[9]

Um die Konstruktionsprinzipien der „Detective Story" wesensmäßig zu erfassen, kommt man allerdings nicht umhin, auch einige soziologische Aspekte der Moderne in seine Betrachtungen mit einzubeziehen.

An erster Stelle zu nennen wäre in diesem Zusammenhang der Wandel im Strafverfahren, der sich mit der Aufklärung vollzog. Während im Mittelalter die Inquisition noch von einer apriorischen Schuld des Beklagten ausging und mit den Mitteln der Folter arbeitete, um ein Geständnis zu erzwingen, ist ein wesentliches Merkmal der Moderne, dass rationale Verfahren der Verbrechensaufklärung ins besondere der Indizienbeweis mehr und mehr in den Vordergrund der Untersuchungen treten. Alewyn wirft in diesem Zusammenhang die Frage auf, ob der Detektivroman nicht geradezu ein Lehrbuch des freiheitlichen Gerichtsverfahrens sei und ob dieser überhaupt entstehen konnte ohne den Wandel im Gerichtswesen.[10]

Verallgemeinert kann man sich wohl auch fragen, ob der Detektivroman ausschließlich in einem demokratischen Umfeld gedeihen kann, da autoritäre Regime eben kein rechtsstaatliches Verfahren kennen. Poe selbst gibt auf diese Fragen keine Antwort. Konstatieren lässt sich allerdings, dass in England 1829 erstmals eine nicht-uniformierte Polizei geschaffen wurde, die mit detektivischen Methoden arbeitete und aus der dann 1842 Scotland Yard hervorging.[11]

---

[9] Alewyn, Richard:Probleme und Gestalten, Der Ursprung des Detektivromans, S. 361-362

[10] Ebd., S. 345

[11] Ebd., S. 345

Poe rekonstruiert allerdings in seinen Erzählungen nicht das polizeiliche Verfahren. Mit der Figur des Dupin kreiert er quasi einen neuen Berufsstand, nämlich den des Privatdetektivs, der in „The..Rue Morgue"[12] scheinbar ohne finanzielle Ambitionen Verbrechensaufklärung betreibt, in „The Purloined Letter" aber schon ganz gezielt einen Lohn für seine Aufklärungsarbeit von dem Präfekten der Stadt Paris einfordert.

Ein weiterer soziologischer Aspekt, der eine unterschwellige aber wichtige Rolle in den Erzählungen spielt, sind Phänomene der Urbanisierung und das Gedeihen von Kriminalität aus der Anonymität der Großstadt heraus.

Besonders in „The Rue Morgue" zeigt sich, dass die Verbrechensaufklärung einem Universum von Unwägbarkeiten und möglichen Kausalitäten ausgesetzt ist, deren Fäden nur schwer mit den Methoden konventioneller Polizeiarbeit zusammenzuführen sind. Die Erkenntnis von Dupin, dass die Würgemale an der ermordeten Mademoiselle L`Espanaye nicht von einem Menschen stammen können, sondern nur von einem Orang-Utan verdeutlicht auf drastische Weise diese Universalität der Möglichkeiten. Erschwerend kommt hinzu, dass es zu Anfang des 19. Jahrhunderts keine sicheren und praktischen Methoden zur Identitätsermittlung gab. Die wissenschaftliche Analyse der Fingerabdrücke wurde 1823 zwar von Purkyne, dem Begründer der Histologie eingeleitet, als kriminalistisches Hilfsmittel wurde es aber erst Ende des 19. Jahrhunderts eingesetzt.[13].

Ein anderer soziologischer Aspekt, der implizit Einfluss auf die Detektivgeschichten Poes hatte, ist das sich rasch entwickelnde Pressewesen.

---

[12] aus Vereinfachungsgründen wurde der Titel verkürzt. (Diese Verfahrensweise führe ich , falls erforderlich fort)

[13] Ginzberg,Carlo:Spurensicherung, S. 44 ff.

E.A. Poe setzte sich in seinem Aufsatz „How to write a Blackwood Article"
intensive mit der sensationshungrigen und oberflächlichen Presse auseinander.
Dort heißt es:

> There was no investigation of first causes, first principles. There was no investigation of anything at all.[14]

Diese Kritik an den Medien, ihre oberflächliche und vorurteilsbeladene
Berichterstattung über Verbrechen spiegelt sich auch in den beiden
Detektivgeschichten wider. Dupin zerlegt, wie ich später nachweisen werde, die
Medienberichterstattung, um dann zu zeigen, wie er zu eigenen und präziseren
Erkenntnissen kommt. In derselben Weise analysiert er die Polizeiarbeit, um
auch dort zu zeigen, wie er zu eigenen und fundierteren Einsichten gelangt.

Das übergeordnete Verfahren, welches sich in den Detektivgeschichten
abzeichnet, ist der Prozess der Wahrheitsfindung, welcher mit einem Rätsel
beginnt und mit der Lösung endet.

Die Rolle des Erzählers

In beiden Erzählungen tritt der Narrator als Ich-Erzähler in Erscheinung, ohne
dass die Identität desselben preisgegeben wird. In „.The Rue Morgue" erfährt
der Leser nur, dass es sich um einen Ausländer handelt, vermutlich um einen
Engländer, der sich vorübergehend in Paris aufhält.

Als Ich-Erzähler ist der Narrator natürlicherweise in die Handlung eingebunden
ohne allerdings die Hauptrolle zu spielen. Seine Aufgabe besteht vielmehr darin,
eine Vermittlerrolle zwischen Dupin und dem Leser herzustellen. In „The Rue
Morgue" zeichnet er zunächst ein differenziertes Charakterbild Dupins um dann

---

[14] Poe,E.A.: How to write a Blackwood Article, S.175

im weiteren Verlauf der Erzählung im Dialog mit seinem Freund dessen Inspirationen, Beobachtungen, Analysen und Schlussfolgerungen zu reflektieren. Der Erzähler selbst besitzt dabei offensichtlich nicht dessen analytische Fähigkeiten. Er zeigt sich oft überrascht von den Beobachtungen und Einsichten Dupins und wirkt manchmal sogar etwas einfältig. Trotzdem scheint beide eine innige und aufrechte Freundschaft zu verbinden. In „The Purloined Letter" hat sich diese Beziehung zwischen dem Erzähler und Dupin zu einem festen Vertrauensverhältnis weiterentwickelt und die gemeinsamen Erfahrungen bei der Aufklärung der Todesfälle in „The Rue Morgue" und „The Murder of Marie Roget" bilden die Basis für die Lösung des nächsten Falls. Trotz dieser Vertrautheit bleibt das Grundmuster der Dialoge dasselbe. Dupin stellt gewagte Hypothesen auf, entwirft extravagante Analogien und kommt zu abenteuerlichen Schlussfolgerungen, während der Erzähler seine offensichtliche Unterlegenheit durch sein exzentrisches Verhalten zu kompensieren sucht.

Diese Charakterisierung des Ich-Erzählers könnte Anlass zu der Vermutung geben, dass dieser quasi die Perspektive des Lesers einnimmt. Warren Hill Kelly vertritt diesen Standpunkt und begründet seine Ansicht mit folgenden Worten:

> Perhaps Poe concluded that the most poignant manner of demonstrating to readers their own insensitivity in reading and their own susceptibility to being led by the nose in interpretation would be to guide them through their own process of reading by means of particular narrative arrangement. [15]

Diese Sichtweise widerspricht zunächst einmal dem Empfinden, dass es sich bei dem Ich-Erzähler um die Stimme des Autors handelt. Zu Beginn der Erzählung „The Murders in the Rue Morgue" ist es der Erzähler und nicht Dupin, der einige Reflexionen über mentale Fähigkeiten der Analyse zum Besten gibt, die sehr differenziert sind und auch im weiteren Verlauf der Story behält er die

---

[15] Kelly, Warren Hill: Detecting the Critic, S.79

Fäden der Erzählung in der Hand, auch wenn der Erkenntnis- und Aufklärungsprozess eindeutig von Dupin betrieben wird. Dennoch spricht auch einiges für die Sichtweise Kellys. So lässt sich nicht erkennen, dass der Erzähler eine kritische oder reflektierte Distanz zu Dupin aufrecht erhält.

Weder stellt er dessen gewagte Hypothesen in Frage noch geht er auf Distanz zu dessen Handlungen, etwa, als Dupin dem Minister den Brief entwendet und durch ein Duplikat ersetzt oder als dieser eigenmächtig den Seemann „vorlädt", um nach polizeilichem Vorbild ein Verhör durchzuführen. Diese unkritische Haltung gegenüber Dupin bis hin zur völligen Identifikation mit dessen Ansichten verleiht dem Erzähler ein gewisses Maß an Unzuverlässigkeit.

Der Mangel an eigenen Beobachtungen und Erkenntnissen zu den Fällen bzw. die mangelnde Fähigkeit zu einem eigenen Urteil lassen daher in der Tat die Vermutung zu, dass die Perspektive des Erzählers weitestgehend mit der Sichtweise eines relativ undifferenzierten Lesers übereinstimmt.

Die Rolle des Auguste Dupin

In „The Rue Morgue" charakterisiert der Erzähler Dupin als einen Menschen, der befähigt ist, Gedanken zu lesen. Es heißt dort:

He boasted to me, with a low chuckling laugh, that most men, in respect to himself, ware windows in their bosoms." [16]

Um dieses Phänomen zu untermauern, schildert der Erzähler folgende Begebenheit: Während beide eines Abends durch die Straßen von Paris spazierten, jeder beschäftigt mit seinen eigenen Gedanken, unterbricht Dupin plötzlich das Schweigen mit den Worten:

---

[16] Poe, E.A.: The Murders in the Rue Morgue, S.. 243

He is a very little fellow, That`s true, and would do better for the Theatre des Varietes."[17]

Offensichtlich hatte Dupin mit diesen Worten genau den Gedanken getroffen, über welchen der Erzähler gerade sinnierte und während dieser noch seine Verwunderung darüber äußerte, ergänzte jener, dass er an Chantilly gedacht habe, einen ehemaligen Schuster, der bühnensüchtig geworden war und der immer wieder versuchte, die Rolle des Xerxes in einer Tragödie Crebillions zu spielen. Dupin besaß also offensichtlich die Fähigkeit des „mind-reading" und setzte diese auch bei seiner Detektivarbeit um.

Weiterhin, so vermittelt der Erzähler, besitzt Dupin eine spezielle analytische Fähigkeit, sehr ausgefallene Rätsel zu lösen. In „The Rue Morgue" heißt es:

He is fond of enigmas, of conundrums, of hieroglyphics; exhibiting in his solutions of each a degree of acumen which appears tot he ordinary apprehension praeternatural.[18]

Er scheint davon überzeugt zu sein, dass die Dinge, die der Polizei und einfachen Leuten mysteriös erscheinen, in irgendeiner Form erklärbar sind. Diese Überzeugung suggeriert Überlegenheit gegenüber den anderen Charakteren der beiden Detektivgeschichten, insbesondere aber auch gegenüber dem Erzähler.

Dupin ist ganz offensichtlich derjenige, der die Entwicklung der Geschichte vorantreibt. Er steuert den Erkenntnisprozess und gibt seine Informationen und Einsichten immer dann weiter, wenn er überzeugt ist, dass der richtige Zeitpunkt dafür gekommen ist. Diese Charakteristik lässt die Frage aufkommen, ob es Anknüpfungspunkte zwischen E.A. Poe als Privatperson und der Figur des Dupin gibt. Warren Hill Kelly vertritt die Auffassung, dass Poe seine eigene

---

[17] Ebd., S.244

[18] Ebd., S.240

kritische Stimme über die Figur des Dupin zur Geltung bringt. Er begründet diese Ansicht mit den Worten:

That mirroring of Poe's critical ideas on readership within the voice of Dupin finds substantiation in the manner in which both Poe's literary technique and content reflect his attitudes toward the readers of his day. [19]

Wie die Ausführungen zu dem Erzähler verdeutlichen, kann diesem eine solche kritische Rolle gegenüber dem Prozess des Erkennens, des Interpretierens und schon gar nicht in Bezug auf die Schlussfolgerungen nachgesagt werden.

Dupin hingegen scheint geeignet zu sein, kritische Reflexionen Poes über den Leser, das Publikum und die Polizeiarbeit zu transportieren.

Er eruiert nicht nur sorgfältiger vor Ort und macht detailliertere Beobachtungen, es ist vor allem der kritische und alles in Frage stellende Umgang mit den vorgegebenen Informationen aus den Medien und die polizeilichen Darstellung der Sachverhalte, die seine Arbeit so erfolgreich macht. Ähnlich wie Poe selbst als Journalist, als Literaturkritiker und als recherchierender Schriftsteller analysiert er die kolportierten Informationen und die häufig voreilig gezogenen Schlussfolgerungen und beweist damit seine Fähigkeit, die an ihn herangetragenen Einschätzungen zu transzendieren und falsche Vorannahmen zu widerlegen. In „The Rue Morgue" beispielsweise analysiert Dupin zunächst zwei Zeitungsberichte zu dem Mordfall, deren Beschreibungen er zwar vor Ort bestätigt findet, welche aber unzureichend sind, weil einige geschulte Beobachtungen, die eigentlich das Ergebnis polizeilicher Ermittlungsarbeit hätten sein müssen, eben nicht gemacht wurden. Andererseits ist er nicht bereit, dass gängige Verdachtsmoment des Geldraubes in Zusammenhang mit dem Mord zu übernehmen, da dieses nicht die unvorstellbare Grausamkeit des

---

[19] Kelly, Warren Hill: (wie Anm. 11) , S. 77

Verbrechens erklären würde. Für Dupin lautet die Schlüsselfrage, wie er gegenüber dem Erzähler räsoniert, nicht, `what has occured`, sondern `what has occured that never has occured before`. [20]

In „The Purloined Letter" sind die Akzente etwas verlagert. Dupin zweifelt in diesem Fall nicht die Sorgfalt der Polizeiarbeit an, im Gegenteil, er verspottet sie, weil er der Meinung ist, dass dieses Verbrechen nicht mit peniblen Hausdurchsuchungen, sondern mit der Kraft des Intellektes zu lösen sei. Dabei kommen theoretische Überlegungen „In the Purloined Letter" zum Tragen, die in der Erzählung „The Murders in the Rue Morgue" bereits entwickelt wurden, nämlich die Technik, den kriminellen Kontrahenten aus der Perspektive eines Spielers zu beobachten. Auf diese Weise gelingt es Dupin, das Verhalten von Minister D zu durchschauen und letztlich zu erkennen, dass dieser gar nicht erst versucht hat, den Brief zu verstecken.

Dabei offenbart sich eine seltsame Wesensgleichheit zwischen Dupin und dem Minister, die sich beide rühmen, sowohl Dichter als auch Mathematiker zu sein. Nur diese Waffengleichheit des Intellekts, so suggeriert die Erzählung, ermöglicht überhaupt die Aufklärung des Verbrechens.

Die Rolle des Präfekten

In „The Rue Morgue" urteilt Dupin über die Polizei:

> The Parisian Police, so much extolled for acumen, are cunning, but not more. There is no method in their proceedings, beyond the method of the moment. [21]

Er präzisiert seine Kritik weiter mit den Worten:

---

[20] Poe, E.A.: (wie Anm. 12) , S. 253

[21] Poe, E.A.: Ebd, S. 251

48

The results attained by them are not unfrequently surprising, but, for the most part, are brought about by simple diligence and activity. When these qualities are availing, their schemes fail. [22]

Über den Präfekten der Pariser Polizei weiß er zu berichten:

Vidoq, for example, was a good guesser, and a persevering man. But, without educated thought, he erred continuously by the very intensity of his investigations. He impaired his vision by holding the object to close. [23]

Diese Statements offenbaren ein gehöriges Maß an Verachtung für den peniblen aber einfallslosen Polizeipräsidenten. In „The Purloined Letter" äußert Dupin seine Kritik nicht nur gegenüber dem Erzähler, sondern verspottet direkt den Präfekten,Monsieur G, der ihn anlässlich des entwendeten Briefes um Rat bittet.

Er lässt den Polizisten die absurd pingelige Durchsuchung des Gebäudes wiederholen, obwohl er längst der Überzeugung ist, dass der Minister gar nicht erst versucht hat, den Brief zu verbergen. Nachdem der Präfekt ihn einen Monat später mit dem Bekenntnis

I could do no more than I have done [24]

erneut um Hilfe bittet, antwortet dieser genüsslich an seiner Meerschaumpfeife ziehend:

G---, you have not exerted yourself – to the utmost in this matter. You might – do a little more, I think, eh?[25]

Gegenüber dem Erzähler treibt Dupin seinen Spott auf die Spitze mit der Bemerkung:

---

[22] Poe, E.A.: Ebd., S. 252

[23] Poe, E.A.: Ebd., S. 252

[24] Poe, E.A.: The Purloined Letter, S. 373

[25] Poe, E.A.: Ebd., S. 373

The measures, then, ... were good in their kind, and well executed; their defect lay in their being inapplicable tot he case and to the men. A certain set of highly ingenious resources are, with the Prefect, a sort of Procrustean bed, to which he forcibly adapts his designs.[26]

Die Dialoge zwischen Dupin und dem Polizisten und die genüsslich-spöttische Präsentation derselben durch den Erzähler offenbaren indirekt auch wie E. A. Poe die Ermittlungsarbeit der Polizei einschätzt. Akzeptiert man dabei die oben zitierte These Kellys, dass Dupin die kritische Stimme des Autors verkörpert, so trifft das sicherlich nicht nur auf das Publikum bzw. seine Zeitgenossen zu, sondern insbesondere auch auf die Polizei.

Einen Aspekt, den E.A. Poe allerdings überhaupt nicht thematisiert, sind sozialpsychologische Erklärungsmuster von kriminellen Verhalten.

Stephan Knight merkt dazu an:

No presentation or analysis oft the social causes of disorder is offered, it is merely suggested that strange and terrible things can happen and a clever man will be able to explain them. The crime an the resolution are without history, without recurring roots. [27]

Damit entgeht der E.A. Poe zwar der Gefahr, sich in das gefährliche Fahrwasser von Vorurteilen zu begeben, andererseits vermitteln seine Detektivgeschichten etwas traumhaft tänzerisches, das sich jenseits der alltäglich erfahrbaren Realität bewegt.

---

[26] Poe, E.A.: Ebd., S. 374

[27] Knight, Stefan: Form and Ideology in Crime Fiction, S.44

Die analytischen Betrachtungen innerhalb der Erzählungen zur Aufdeckung eines Verbrechens

Einen ersten Einblick in die Logik der Erzählungen und damit in die Denkweise E.A. Poes wird im ersten Absatz von „The Murders in the Rue Morgue" vermittelt. Dort heißt es:

> „As the strong man exults in his physical ability, delighting in such exercises as call his muscles into action, so glories the analyst in that moral activity which disentangles....He is fond of enigmas, of conundrums, of hieroglyphics; exhibiting in his solutions of each a degree of acumen which appears to the ordinary apprehension preternatural. His results, brought about by the very soul and essence of method, have, in truth, the whole air of intuition. [28]

Ein Analyst, so der Erzähler, ist also jemand, der ein Rätsel oder eine Hieroglyphe zu lösen hat. In einem Aufsatz in „The Literati of New York City" präzisiert E. Allen Poe diesen Gedanken:

> „The soul is a cipher, in the sense of a cryptograph..." [29]

Dabei ist der Ausdruck, dass die Seele eine Geheimschrift im Sinne eines Kryptografen sei, nicht nur als eine Metapher zu verstehen. Poe beschäftigte sich intensiv mit der Entschlüsselung von Geheimschriften, insbesondere mit der zu seiner Zeit spektakulären Entschlüsselung der ägyptischen Hieroglyphen durch den Orientalisten Champollion. Irving führt dazu aus:

> „Of the major writers oft the American Renaissance ‚Poe, was the one for whom Champollion, in his role as a decipherer of cryptic writing, had the greatest personal significance. He became for Poe a kind of model of scientific intuition as opposed to the drudgeries of inductive and deductive reasoning." [30]

---

[28] Poe E.A.: (wie Anm. 12), S.240

[29] Irwin, T. John: American Hieroglyphics, The Hieroglyphics an d the Quest for Origins, S.43

[30] Ebda , S. 43

Die Entschlüsselung eines Kryptografen ist für Poe einerseits ein wissenschaftliches Verfahren, welches er beispielsweise in der Erzählung „The Gold-Bug"[31] explizit vorführt, anderseits mystifiziert er diese Vorgehensweise, da eine Geheimschrift seiner Meinung nach nicht allein durch deduktive oder induktive Methoden zu enträtseln sei, sondern durch Intuition. Dieser Gedanke lässt sich auch in „The Purloined Letter" nachweisen, denn Dupin weist darauf hin, dass sein Kontrahent, Minister D, sowohl Mathematiker als auch Poet sei, also sowohl Meister einer streng naturwissenschaftlichen Methode wie beispielsweise der Differenzialrechnung als auch ein intuitiv und kreativ arbeitender Dichter. Damit lässt sich in einer ersten Annäherung erschließen, welches Anforderungsprofil eines Detektivs den Erzählungen zugrunde liegt.

Ein Detektiv hat demnach die Seele eines Verbrechers wie eine Geheimschrift zu enträtseln, indem er sich sowohl mathematischer Verfahren als auch der Intuition bedient. Dieser Denkansatz entbehrt allerdings nicht einer gewissen Tücke, da mit Galilei das Motto "individuum est ineffabile"[32] als Paradigma für eine antianthropozentrische Sichtweise in den Naturwissenschaften zu Poes Zeit noch weitestgehend unangefochten galt. Begründet wurde und wird diese Sichtweise folgendermaßen:

> Tatsächlich implizieren der Gebrauch der Mathematik und die experimentelle Methode die Quantifizierung bzw. die Wiederholbarkeit der Dinge, während eine individualisierende Wissenschaftsrichtung die Wiederholbarkeit per Definition ausschloss und die Quantifizierung nur als Hilfsfunktion zuließ. [33]

In diesem Sinne ließen sich mathematische Verfahren als Hilfsfunktion nur auf die Technik des Indizienbeweises anwenden. Ginsberg konstatiert dazu:

---

[31] Poe, E.A.: The Gold Bug, S. 321-348

[32] Ginzburg, Carlo: (Wie Anm. 9), S.24

[33] Ebda, S. 24

„Zwischen 1870 und 1880 begann sich in den Humanwissenschaften ein Indizienparadigma durchzusetzen, das sich (eben)auf die Semiotik stützte." [34]

Diese Verfahrensweise des Indizienbeweises etablierte sich demnach erst 25 Jahre nach E.A. Poes Tod. Im weiteren Verlauf der Erzählungen zeigt sich,dass es Poe zwar auch um Indizien ging, schwerpunktmäßig aber eben um die Entschlüsselung der Seele des kriminellen Kontrahenten, die es wie eine Hieroglyphe zu enträtseln galt. Es überrascht daher auch nicht, dass in den Erzählungen nichtmathematische Techniken herangezogen werden, um das kriminelle Gedankengerüst des Gegners zu entwirren. In „The Rue Morgue" etwa wägt der Erzähler die Strategien eines Schachspielers oder die Spielstrategien von Kartenspielern ab, um daraus Möglichkeiten der Detektion abzuleiten. Auch diesbezüglich lässt sich anmerken, dass die Strategien von Spielern schon zu Zeiten Poes Eingang in mathematische Untersuchungen zur Spieltheorie gefunden haben. So veröffentlichte Bernoulli im Jahr 1713 seine „Ars conjectandi", die Kunst der Vermutung, welche die moderne Theorie der Probabilität begründet hat:

„Die Erfinder der Glücksspiele, schreibt Bernoulli, hätten, ohne es selbst zu wissen, Meßapparaturen der Wahrscheinlichkeit erfunden: Erst fertigten sie Vorrichtungen zur Erzeugung gleich wahrscheinlicher Ereignisse an, (zum Beispiel die Hardware der Würfel), dann legten sie Zeichen für die Bestimmung von Gewinn und Verlust fest (die Software der auf ihnen aufgetragenen Ziffern).[35]

Wie sich zeigt, geht es Poe bei seiner Betrachtung von Spielstrategien allerdings nicht darum, Messapparaturen der Wahrscheinlichkeit in die Techniken der Detektion zu integrieren. Vielmehr analysiert er die Kraft des reflektierenden Intellekts eines Spielers bei der Beobachtung seines Gegners. Der Erzähler in

---

[34] Ebda, S. 17

[35] Campe, Rüdiger: Spiel der Wahrscheinlichkeit S. 21

„The Rue Morgue" erläutert an dem Beispiel eines Kartenspielers, was er darunter versteht:

„He (the player) examines the countenance of his partner, comparing it carefully with that of each of his opponents. He considers the mode of assorting the cards in each hand; often counting trump by trump, and honour by honour, through the glances bestowed by their holders upon each. He notes every variation of face as the play progresses, gathering a fund of thought from the differences in the expression of certainty, of surprise, of triumph, or chagrin....He recognizes what is played through feint, by the air with which it is thrown upon the table. A casual or inadvertent word; the accidental dropping or turning of a card, with the accompanying anxiety or carelessness in regard to its concealment....." [36]

Übersetzt man diese Betrachtungen in das Anforderungsprofil eines Detektivs, so wird deutlich, dass es Poe weniger um ein wahrscheinlichkeitstheoretisches Kalkül geht als vielmehr um die Fähigkeit den Gegner auf Grund psychologischer, physiognomischer und phrenologischer Beobachtungen „berechenbar" zu machen. Sowohl die physiognomische als auch die phrenologische Methode unterstellen dabei, dass die äußere Erscheinung einer Person die ihr inne wohnende Eigenschaften offenbart. Erzählungen wie „The Gold Bug" [37] verdeutlichen, wie sehr Poe von den Möglichkeiten dieser Techniken überzeugt war. Heutige wissenschaftstheoretische Untersuchungen stellen die Möglichkeiten der Physiognomie und insbesondere der Phrenologie erheblich in Frage. G.R. Thompson beispielsweise bezeichnet in dem Kapitel „Sciences of the Mind" [38] sowohl die Physiognomie als auch die Phrenologie als pseudowissenschaftliche Verfahren. Auch Ginsberg [39] spricht von einem schnellen Niedergang der Phrenologie als Wissenschaft. Am Ende der einleitenden Assoziationen in „The Rue Morgue" zur Analyse des Menschen

---

[36] Poe, E.A.: (wie Anm. 12) S.241-242

[37] Poe, E.A. (wie Anm. 27) S. 321-348

[38] Thompson, G.R. : Selected Writings of Edgar Allen Poe, Sciences of the Mind, S. 742

[39] Ginzburg, Carlo: (Wie Anm. 9) , S. 39

bzw. der Entschlüsselung seiner Seele relativiert der Erzähler seine weitschweifigen Spekulationen ein wenig, indem er konstatiert, dass es wohl ein Irrtum sei, dass die Phrenologen der Erfindungsgabe ein eigenes Organ zuordnen, besteht aber darauf, dass zwischen Erfindungsreichtum und den analytischen Fähigkeiten ein himmelweiter Unterschied bestünde und dass beide Fähigkeiten für einen Detektiv unabdingbar sind.[40]

Durchgesetzt hat sich hingegen ein halbes Jahrhundert nach dem Tode Poes mit Sigmund Freud die psychologische Analyse des Menschen. Abgeleitet aus dem medizinischen Modell der Semiotik entwickelte Freud die Psychoanalyse, die auch heute noch mit der Motivforschung und der Psychopathologie einen wichtigen Beitrag zur Kriminalistik leistet. In „The Purloined Letter" ist es hauptsächlich Dupin, der sich grundsätzliche Gedanken über die Fähigkeiten und Herausforderungen macht, denen sich ein Detektiv zu stellen hat. Auch in dieser Erzählung wird die Enträtselung der Seele des kriminellen Kontrahenten in den Vordergrund gestellt. So philosophiert Dupin darüber, dass Minister D sowohl Poet als auch Mathematiker sei und konstatiert nicht ohne Eitelkeit, dass, wäre D nur Mathematiker, er nicht alles hätte perfekt planen können und der Gnade des Präfekten hoffnungslos ausgeliefert wäre. Diese merkwürdige Schlussfolgerung begründet er damit, dass:

„Mathematical axioms are not axioms of general truth. What is true of relation –of form and quantity –is often grossly false in regard to morals, ...

There are numerous other mathematical truths which are only truth within the limits of relation. But the mathematician argues, from finite truth, through habit, as if they were of an absolutely general applicability- as the world indeed imagines them to be."[41]

---

[40] Poe, E.A. (wie Anm. 12) S. 242

[41] Poe, E.A.: (wie Anm. 20) S. 377

Denkt man diesen Gedanken zu Ende, so behauptet Dupin nicht mehr und nicht weniger, als dass ein Mathematiker kein perfektes Verbrechen planen könne, weil mathematische Aussagesysteme nur einen beschränkten Eigenschafts- bzw. Ereignisraum erschließen und damit nie die ganze Wirklichkeit abbilden. Diese Aussage würde sicherlich von jedem Mathematiker akzeptiert werden, dennoch wirft sie auch ein merkwürdiges Licht auf Dupin und seine Intentionen in dieser Geschichte. Im weiteren Verlauf seiner Überlegungen abstrahiert Dupin seinen Gedankengang und schlägt mit folgenden Worten eine Brücke zur Poesie:

„The material world...abounds with very strict analogies to the immaterial; and thus some colour of truth has been given to the rhetorical dogma, that metaphor, or simile, may be made to strengthen an argument, as well as to embellish a description....“[42]

Die Poesie ist damit das Reich, welches die Schranken der Mathematik aufhebt und den Analytiker beziehungsweise den Detektiv in die Lage versetzt, kraft Intuition und Erfindungsreichtum die Situation in ihrer ganzen Komplexität zu erfassen. Tatsächlich ist es dann auch wieder ein Spiel, welches sich bei Kindern großer Beliebtheit erfreut, das Dupin auf die richtige Fährte führt.

Bei diesem Spiel geht es darum, einen von einer Spielpartei vorgegebenen Namen eines Flusses, einer Stadt oder eines Staates auf einer Karte zu finden.

Dupin behauptet, dass ein professioneller Spieler im Gegensatz zu einem Neuling einen Namen suchen lässt, der sich in großen Lettern über die ganze Karte erstreckt, da sich die Gegenpartei erfahrungsgemäß auf das klein Gedruckte konzentrieren würde.

---

[42] Poe, E.A.: Ebda S. 378

56

Er überträgt diesen Gedanken auf die vorgegebene Herausforderung, den entwendeten Brief zu finden und kommt zu dem vermeintlich banalen Schluss, dass Minster D den Brief ganz bewusst nicht versteckt und wie ein x-beliebiges Schriftstück herum liegen lässt, um auf diese Weise den akribischen Untersuchen der Polizei zu entgehen. Dieser unsystematische und der freien Assoziation zu einem Spiel entstammende Gedanke führt dann letztlich nicht nur zum Erfolg, sondern er karikiert auch die penible aber gedankenlose Suche des Präfekten und seiner Gehilfen nach dem entwendeten Brief.

Wirkungsabsicht und Rezeption der beiden Erzählungen

Welche Schlussfolgerungen lassen Poes Äußerungen als Lektor, Kritiker und Theoretiker in Bezug auf seine Wirkungsabsicht zu?

Die wichtigste Intention, die man wohl jedem Schriftsteller, der Detektivgeschichten schreibt, unterstellen darf, ist, dass er Neugier und Spannung erzeugen möchte.

E. A. Poe stellt dabei, wie er selbst in „The Philosophy of Composition" konstatiert, den zu erzielenden Effekt [43] in den Vordergrund seiner Überlegungen. und betont, dass die Einheitlichkeit des Gesamteindrucks nur dann erreicht werden kann, wenn das literarische Werk in einem Stück gelesen wird. Nur so könne die Totalität der Wirkung gewahrt werden.[44]

Diese Betonung des Effekts lässt die Frage aufkommen, welches ästhetisches Selbstverständnis Poes Werken zugrunde liegt. Der Begriff Ästhetik selbst war zu Poes Zeit besonders im englischsprachigen Raum nur wenig etabliert. Im deutschsprachigen Raum hatte Baumgarten 1750 seinen Aufsatz „Ästhetica" veröffentlicht und Emanuel Kant publizierte 1790 seine „Kritik der ästhetischen Urteilskraft". Diese beiden Werke entfesselten eine lebhafte Diskussion in Philosophie und Kunst über den Geschmack und das Schöne. Im englischen Sprachraum, so konstatiert Rachel Polonsky, wurde der noch junge Begriff Ästhetik mit Skepsis aufgenommen:

… as a silly pedantic term … one of the metaphysical and useless additions to nomenclature in the arts in which the German writers abound. [45]

---

[43] Poe, E.A.: (wie Anm 1), S. 676

[44] Poe, E.A.: Ebda, S. 677

[45] Polonsky, Rachel: Poe`s aesthetic Theory, S. 43

Die Poeten der englischen Romantik des frühen 19. Jahrhunderts besannen sich mehr auf den kreativen Prozess des Poeten selbst als auf ästhetische Betrachtungen des Werkes und befrachteten den Schaffensprozess des Dichters mit theologischen, moralischen und didaktischen Attituden.

E.A. Poe sah sich unausweichlich dieser Denkrichtung ausgesetzt, entwickelte aber mit „The Poetic Principle" und „The Philosophy of Composition" recht eigenständige Gedanken zu der Thematik. In „The Poetic Principle" propagiert er thesenhaft:

> We have taken it into our heads that to write a poem simply for the poem's sake and to acknowledge such to have been our design, would be to confess ourselves radically wanting in the true poetic dignity and force: — but the simple fact is that would we but permit ourselves to look into our own souls we should immediately there discover that under the sun there neither exists nor can exist any work more thoroughly dignified, more supremely noble, than this very poem, this poem per se, this poem which is a poem and nothing more, this poem written solely for the poem's sake.[46]

Mit diesem Ausspruch kommt E.A. Poe den Axiomen der Ästhetik, wie sie von Baumgarten und Kant propagiert wurden, recht nahe und befindet sich gleichzeitig in Einklang mit den „L´art pour l´art-Protagonisten" wie Gautier, Baudelaire oder T.S. Elliot. Allerdings muss man einschränkend feststellen, dass Poe das „Art-for-arts-sake-Paradigma" in seiner literarischen Praxis nicht durchhalten kann. Insbesondere in seinen Detektivgeschichten und in seinem Aufsatz „The Philosophy of Composition" offenbart sich, dass dem Autor zwar die Befreiung des kreativen Schaffens von didaktischen, theologischen und ähnlichen Ansprüchen gelungen ist, allerdings schränkt er diesen neu gewonnen Freiheitsraum wieder ein, indem er sich selbst einen ideologischen Zwang der Methode auferlegt. Wie bereits erwähnt, verlangt er von sich selbst, ein Gedicht oder eine Kurzgeschichte mit der logischen Strenge der Mathematik zu

---

[46] Poe, E.A.: From the Poetic Principle, S. 700

konstruieren oder quasi mechanische Verfahren zu etablieren und sich nicht von einem Zwischenfall oder einem bemerkenswerten Ereignis bei dem Aufbau einer Erzählung leiten zu lassen. Im Grunde genommen verwirft er den Versuch eines ästhetischen Prinzips und konzipiert stattdessen eine ästhetische „Technologie", die Kunst unter den Primat des Machens stellt.[47]. Der Auffassung von Kunst als Intuition widersetzt er sich dabei mit aller Entschiedenheit. Stattdessen betont er die handwerkliche Dimension von Dichtung und die Aufgabe Wahrheit zu vermitteln. In „The Poetic Principle" konkretisiert er diesen Gedanken mit den Worten:

> In enforcing a truth, we need severity rather than efflorescence of language. We must be simple, precise, terse. We must be cool, calm, unimpassioned. In a word, we must be in that mood which, as nearly as possible, is the exact converse of the poetical.[48]

Konfrontiert man diesen Anspruch mit seinen Erzählungen, dann erstaunt es, wie viel Fantasie den Geschichten zugrunde liegt, wie sehr das Unwahrscheinliche und das weit von aller Vorstellung entfernt liegende kausal relevant wird und wie viel Bedeutung dem Rätselhaften zukommt.

Für seine Detektivgeschichten erscheint es ihm besonders wichtig, das Ende der Erzählung fest im Auge zu haben, bevor man überhaupt anfängt zu schreiben. Alle Ereignisse, Vorfälle und Handlungen haben sich der Entwicklung zu diesem Endpunkt (denouement)[49] unterzuordnen, um den gewünschten Effekt zu erzielen, den Leser zu fesseln, zu überraschen und zu verblüffen.

---

[47] Gregorzewski, Carl: E.A.Poe und die Anfänge einer originär amerikanischen Ästhetik, S. 238

[48] Poe, E.A.: (wie Anm. 42), S. 700

[49] Poe, E.A. : (Wie Anm.1), S. 675

Welche Wirkungen haben die Erzählungen auf den Leser?

Ob es dem Autor tatsächlich gelungen ist, die oben zitierte Wirkung zu erzielen, lässt sich einerseits aus der subjektive Erfahrung heraus abschätzen und andererseits natürlich auch als Indikator aus der Auflagenstärke seiner „Detective Stories". Es dürfte wenig Zweifel bestehen, dass er es geschafft hat, den Leser zu fesseln, zu überraschen und zu verblüffen.

Ursache für diesen Erfolg ist einerseits sicherlich, dass die Erzählungen in einer Sitzung gelesen werden können. Poe selbst begründet die Kürze seiner Detektivgeschichten folgendermaßen:

> If any literary work is too long to be read at one sitting, we must be content to dispense with the immensely important effect, derivable from unity of impression – for, if two sittings be required, the affairs of the world interfere, and anything like totality is at once destroyed.[50]

Die Totalität des ersten Eindrucks nutzt der Autor also, um den Leser zu überrumpeln und der Suggestivkraft seiner Erzählung zu unterwerfen. Doch diese Tatsache allein reicht nicht aus, den gewünschten Effekt zu erklären.

Es ist vor allem die innovative Art, einen Kriminalfall als ein Rätsel darzustellen, als eine intellektuelle Herausforderung, der die Polizei offensichtlich nicht gewachsen ist. Der Leser wird aus der vertrauten Perspektive des Voyeurs herausgerissen und dazu angeregt, sich an der Aufklärung des Verbrechens zu beteiligen. Er sieht sich vor die Aufgabe gestellt, die von der Presse kommunizierten Informationen kritisch zu hinterfragen, die gängigen Vorurteile zu überwinden und seine vertrauten aber fragwürdigen Erklärungsmuster zu transzendieren. Dennoch ist der Autor weit davon entfernt, seine Leser zu einer kritischen Haltung zu erziehen. Solch einem

---

[50] Poe, E.A.: (Wie Anm.1), S. 677

didaktischen Ansinnen erteilt Poe in „The Poetik Principle"[51] eine klare Absage. Wichtiger ist es ihm, wie er in dem selben Aufsatz sagt, die Seele zu begeistern und in höhere Sphären zu führen.[52]

Überraschend ist auch, dass die Erzählungen die Spannung nicht aus der Handlung heraus entwickeln, etwa durch Inszenierung einer Verfolgungsjagd, in der die Protagonisten sich abenteuerlichen Herausforderungen gegenüber gestellt sehen. Vielmehr handelt es sich eher um eine Denksportaufgabe mit ausgesprochen vielen spekulativen Elementen, die es aus der „Armchair-Perspektive" heraus zu lösen gilt. Die Dialoge zwischen Dupin und dem Erzähler vermitteln dabei eine Leidenschaft für den akademischen Diskurs, die weit über die Erfordernisse der Detektion hinaus gehen. Das Vergnügen an wissenschaftstheoretischen und ästhetischen Fragestellungen überlagert teilweise die Aufklärungsarbeit dermaßen, dass eine skurrile Kluft zu den dargestellten Realitäten entsteht.

Adressat der beiden Detektivgeschichten dürfte daher der gehobene Mittelstand sein, der auch in der Lage ist, diese Diskurse nachzuvollziehen. Für diesen Leserkreis spricht auch die Tatsache, dass E.A. Poe, anders als Charles Dickens, völlig auf sozialpsychologische und soziologische Erklärungsmuster verzichtet.

Welche Grundstrukturen finden sich in späteren Detektivgeschichten anderer Autoren wieder?

Schon im 18. Jahrhundert gab es zahlreiche Kriminalerzählungen. Diese hatten jedoch einen völlig anderen Charakter als die des 19. und 20. Jahrhunderts. Das lag vor allem daran, dass im 18. Jahrhundert das Strafsystem völlig anders

---

[51] Poe, E.A.: (Wie Anm. 42) , S. 700

[52] Poe, E.A.: (Wie Anm.42), S. 698

geartet war, dass es kein zuverlässiges Polizeisystem gab, ganz zu schweigen von einem System der Detektion. Die Strafverfolgung war noch eine Aufgabe der verletzten Partei und das Hauptwerkzeug der Rechtsdurchsetzung waren Horrorstrafen.

Für viele Erzähler des 18. Jahrhunderts war die Quelle ihrer Kriminalgeschichten das Gefängnis Newgate in London bzw. die Aufzeichnungen über die dort einsitzenden Verbrecher in dem sog. Newgate-Kalender. Defoe`s „Jack Sheppard" ist ein Beispiel für diese Novellen. Diese Erzählungen waren jedoch nicht an eine bestimmte Form gebunden oder an ein näher definiertes Publikum gerichtet, wie dies in den Detektivgeschichten des 19. Jahrhunderts der Fall war. Die Grundkonstruktion eines privat ermittelnden Detektivs in Verbindung mit einem Assistenten, fand seine bekannteste Ausprägung in den Figuren des Sherlock Holmes und Dr. Watson von Arthur Conan Doyle. Ähnlich wie die Figur des Dupin glänzt Sherlock Holmes durch seine exzentrische Lebensweise, er raucht Kokain, spielt eine Stradivari und führt dandyhaft philosophische Gespräche mit Watson. Anderseits besticht er bei seinen forensischen Untersuchungen ähnlich wie der Protagonist Poes durch detailgenaue Beobachtungen und nüchterne Schlussfolgerungen. In „A Study in Scarlet" bezieht sich die Figur des Sherlock Holmes im Dialog mit Watson sogar auf E.A. Poes Dupin und kanzelt diesen mit der ihm eigenen Arroganz mit den Worten „He had some analytical genius, no doubt; but he was by no means such a phenomenon as Poe appeared to imagine." [53] ab. Die Detektivgeschichten Doyles sind also nach dem gleichen Konzept aufgebaut, wie Poes Dupin-Erzählungen, wobei allerdings der geographische und soziologisch-politische

---

[53] Doyle, Arthur Conan: A Study in Scarlet, Chapter 2 – The Science of Deduction, S. 2

Bezugsrahmen nicht Frankreich bzw. Paris ist, sondern das viktorianisch geprägte London des späten 19. Jahrhunderts.

Die Sherlock Holmes-Erzählungen waren erheblich erfolgreicher als die „Detective Stories" von E.A. Poe, rein äußerlich daran abzulesen, dass Doyle insgesamt drei Romane und vierundzwanzig Kurzgeschichten mit der Starfigur des Detektivs schrieb. Sherlock Holmes wurde damit zum ersten Serienhelden dieses Genres dank der von Poe vorgedachten Ideen und seines Konstruktionsschemas.

Schluss

Die Detektivgeschichte als Paradigma eines neuen Genres

Als Resümee lässt sich fest halten, dass neben der Figurenkonstellation die Betrachtung eines Kriminalfalles aus der Perspektive des abstrahierenden Analytikers das bestimmende Element von Poes Erzählungen war. Wesensmerkmale der Aufklärung spiegeln sich in den Erzählungen ebenso wider, wie der sich abzeichnende Aufbruch in den Naturwissenschaften. Poe kontrastiert die von ihm erfahrene Moderne mit dem Schaurigen und dem Abgründigen wie schon vorher in seinen „Gothic Tales" und bringt als besonderes kompositorisches Element die Beschäftigung mit kryptischen Rätseln ein. Die Verherrlichung des überlegenen analytischen Geistes findet sich noch einmal in den Detektivgeschichten um Sherlock Holmes wieder, wurde aber in späteren Erzählungen nicht mehr in dieser übertriebenen satirischen Form praktiziert. Stattdessen haben viele wissenschaftliche Verfahren als gesicherte Erkenntnis Eingang in die Forensik gefunden und sind damit auch nach wie vor Thema moderner Detektivgeschichten. Die mystische Verklärung des analytischen Verfahrens ist dabei längst einer nüchternen Rationalität gewichen, auch wenn neue Techniken, wie DNA-Analyse oder Möglichkeiten der Datenbeschaffung mittels moderner EDV-Systeme dem Leser oder Zuschauer auch heute noch eine Aura vermitteln, die die Allmacht der Wissenschaft unangefochten lässt. Auch die Methode des psychologischen Ausleuchtens des kriminellen Kontrahenten hat längst Eingang gefunden in die Kriminologie und ist mittels eines sog. Profilers fester Bestandteil der Verbrechensbekämpfung.

Anders als im 18. Jahrhundert integrieren viele moderne Detektivgeschichten dabei wieder komplexe und spannende Handlungselemente in das Verfahren der Detektion und beschränken sich nicht mehr auf die passive reflektierende

Rolle des Detektivs. Die idealtypische Konstellation, die Poe mit seinen Detektivgeschichten vorgegeben hat, findet sich daher hauptsächlich bei „Sherlock Holmes" wieder. Schon Agatha Christie verzichtete auf die „Armchair-Perspektive" und ließ ihren Detektiv Poirot ausgedehnte Reisen unternehmen und spannende handlungsorientierte Abenteuer bei der Aufklärung seiner Verbrechen erleben. Vor allem bei der filmischen Umsetzung von „Detektive Stories" gibt man heute den handlungsorientierten Erzählungen den Vorzug.

Literaturangaben

Sammelbände

The Selected Writings of Edgar Allen Poe. Hg. von G. R. Thompson. New York und London 2004

Daraus:

Primärtexte:

How to write a Blackwood Article, S. 173-183

The Murders in the Rue Morgue , S. 239-266

The Gold Bug, S. 321-348

The Purloined Letter, S. 367-382

The Philosophy of Composition, S. 675-685

From The Poetic Principle, S. 698-704

Daraus:

Sekundärtexte:

Armstrong, Liahna: The Shadows Shadow: The Motif of the Double in Edgar Allen Poe`s "The Purloined Letter", S. 863-873

Fowler, Orson S.: Fowlers Practical Phrenology, S. 745-746

Riddel, N. Joseph: The "Crypt" of Edgar Poe, S. 884-896

Spurzheim, Johann G.: The Physiognomical System of Dr.Gall and Spurzheim. S. 742-743

The Cambridge Companion to Edgar Allen Poe.Hg von Kevon J. Hayes. Cambridge 2002

Daraus:

Polonsky, Rachel: Poe`s aesthetic Theory, S. 42-56

Thoms, Peter: Poe`s Dupin and the Power of Detection, S. 133-146

The Cambridge Companion to Crime Fiction. Hg von Martin Priestman. Cambridge 2003.

Daraus:

Bell, Ian A.: Eigtheenth-Century Crime Writing, S. 7-18

Kayman, Martin A.: The Short-Story from Poe to Chesterton, S. 41-58

Pykett, Lyn: The Newgate Novel and Sensation Fiction 1830-1868, S. 19- 40

Einzelwerke:

Alewyn, Richard: Probleme und Gestalten. Ursprung des Detektivromans. Frankfurt a.M 1974, S.341-360

Alewyn, Richard: Probleme und Gestalten. Anatomie des Detektivromans.

Frankfurt a. M 1974, S.341-394

Aristoteles: Poetik. Stuttgart 1982

Doyle, Arthur, Conan: A Study in Scarlet. The Science of Deduction. www.Literatur.org 7.7.2008, S.2

Ginzburg, Carlo: Spurensicherung. Die Wissenschaft auf der Suche nach sich selbst. Berlin 2002, S. 7-57

Gregorzewski, Carla: Edgar Allen Poe und die Anfänge einer originär amerikanischen Ästhetik. Heidelberg 1982

Irwin, T. John: American Hieroglyphics. The Symbol oft he Egyptian Hieroglyphics in the American Renaissance. New Haven und London 1980, S. 43-223

Kampe,Rüdiger: Spiel der Wahrscheinlichkeit. Literatur und Berechnung zwischen Pascal und Kleist. Göttingen 2002, S. 21-41

Knight, Stephen: Form and Ideology in Crime Fiction. London and Basingstoke 1980, S. 39-66

Kreuzer, Helmut: Mathematik und Dichtung. Versuche zur Frage einer exakten Literaturwissenschaft. München 1965, S. 9-21

Zeitschriftenartikel

Kelly, Warren Hill: Detecting the Critic. The Presence of Poe's Critical Voice in His Stories of Dupin, Ellen A. Poe Review (EAPR) 2003, S. 77-86

Ines Sundermann (2007): "You remind me of Edgar Allan Poe's Dupin". C. Auguste Dupin und Sherlock Holmes im Vergleich

Einleitung

Wenn wir an einen Vater aller literarischen Detektive denken, dann kommt uns meist Sherlock Holmes in den Sinn. Die Figur gilt als Vorlage späterer namhafter Detektive, der Name fast schon als Synonym für „Detektiv". Die vom englischen Schriftsteller Sir Arthur Conan Doyle erfundene Figur erlangte solch einen Erfolg, dass sie vielfach und in allen erdenkbaren Medienformaten parodiert, imitiert und rekonstruiert wurde (vgl. Knight 1980, 67). Der erste im Jahre 1887 veröffentlichte Holmes-Roman *A Study in Scarlet* schlug „*wie eine Bombe auf dem Gebiet der Detektivliteratur ein*" (Sayers 1977, 169). Der Erfolg machte Doyle reich, zwang ihn aber auch, seine Holmes-Geschichten fortzuführen, obwohl er sich lieber mit anderem beschäftigt hätte (vgl. Knight 1980, 67).

Oft bleibt vergessen, dass Sherlock Holmes nicht der Ursprung aller großen Detektive der Literatur war, hatte er doch selbst eine noch ältere Detektivfigur als Vorbild: C. Auguste Dupin, der schon 1841 in drei Kurzgeschichten des amerikanischen Schriftstellers Edgar Allan Poe ermittelt. Doyle schreibt selbst: „*Poe's masterful detective, M. Dupin, had from boyhood been one of my heroes.*" (Doyle 1944, 47) Poe sei „*'der Vater der Detektivgeschichte'*", es schiene unmöglich, dass „*'Nachahmer irgendwo Neuland erschließen könnten, das sie mit voller Überzeugung als ihr eigen anzusehen vermöchten.'*" (Matthews 1977, 51 f). In *A Study In Scarlet* findet sich auch eine Referenz, als Holmes' Freund Watson dem Detektiv gegenüber bemerkt: „*You remind me of Edgar Allen [sic] Poe's Dupin*" (Doyle 2004, 16). Dennoch wird der Holmes-Figur so viel Eigenständigkeit zugeschrieben, dass spätere Detektive der englischen Literatur in der Regel auf ihn und nicht auf Dupin zurückgeführt werden. (vgl. Becker 1975, 11 f)

Anhand Poes erster Dupin-Geschichte „The Murders in the Rue Morgue", die erstmals 1841 in *Graham's Magazine* erschienen ist (vgl. Poe 2004, 239), und Doyles erster Holmes-Geschichte „A Study in Scarlet" (erstmals erschienen in *Beeton's Christmas Annual of 1887*, vgl. Doyle 2004, VIII), werde ich im Folgenden überprüfen, wo die Gemeinsamkeiten und die Unterschiede zwischen C. Auguste Dupin und Sherlock Holmes liegen. Ich werde dabei auf die Darstellung der beiden Detektivfiguren, insbesondere auf ihre detektivischen Methoden, und auf die jeweiligen Beziehungen zwischen den Erzählern und den Detektiven eingehen. Da es sich anbietet, werde ich zudem die Erzählperspektiven miteinander vergleichen. So lässt sich insgesamt feststellen, wo sich Doyle an Poe orientierte und wo nicht, d. h. wie viel Eigenständigkeit die Holmes-Figur besitzt.

Figurendarstellung

Persönlichkeit

Die Persönlichkeit der Hauptfigur Dupin wird uns durch die Erzählung des namenlosen Chronisten der Geschichte vermittelt. Durchweg wird uns ein unglaublich analytisches Genie vor Augen gehalten. Der Effekt wird einerseits erzielt durch die bloße Handlung: Sie verläuft immer zu Dupins Gunsten, mit seinen Schlussfolgerungen trifft er immer ins Schwarze. Andererseits untermauern die direkten Reaktionen des Erzählers auf die geistigen Kunststücke von Dupin das Bild des Genies. Immer wieder bringt er seine Überwältigung zum Ausdruck: „*'Dupin,' said I gravely, ‚this is beyond my comprehension. I do not hesitate to say that I am amazed, and can scarcely credit my senses. How was it possible you should know I was thinking of –?'*" (Poe 1994, 123) oder "*I stared at the speaker [Dupin] in mute astonishment*" (ebd., 135).

Der Franzose Dupin stammt aus einer aristokratischen Familie, geriet jedoch durch gewisse Umstände in Armut und unternahm keine Anstrengungen, seine finanzielle Lage zu ändern, „*Books, indeed, were his sole luxuries*" (Poe 1994, 121). Nicht nur hier wird deutlich, dass soziale Werte für ihn keine Rolle spielen. Auch das Ausbleiben einer Kritik an dem Halter des Orang-Utans, der durch die Züchtigung des Tieres die Tötung in der Rue Morgue mitzuverschulden hat (vgl. ebd., 150 f), lassen erkennen, dass es Dupin nicht an der Aufrechterhaltung einer sozialen Ordnung liegt. Zwar revanchiert sich Dupin durch seine Mithilfe an dem Fall bei dem zu Unrecht inhaftierten Le Bon für einen Gefallen, den ihm dieser einst getan hat, was eine soziale Ader vermuten lässt, doch der Hauptimpuls für seine Detektivarbeit ist bloßes Vergnügen an der Sache selbst: „*[Dupin] is motivated by the specific intellectual problem, rather than by social or ethical values. [Because] much of the tale is taken up by lengthy discussions of his psychological, analytic and linguistic theories."* (Kayman 2003, 45) „*'An inquiry will afford us amusement'"* (Poe 1994, 133), sagt Dupin selbst, Le Bon erwähnt er erst an zweiter Stelle. Auch sein Gefährte bemerkt: *"He seemed, too, to take an eager delight in [it] [...] and did not hesitate to confess the pleasure thus derived."* (ebd., 123)

Dupin und gewisse Beamte der örtlichen Polizei kennen sich zwar gegenseitig, er selbst ist jedoch kein offiziell von der Polizei beschäftigter, sondern ein Amateur-Detektiv. Seinen Lebensunterhalt bestreitet Dupin daher nicht durch die Detektivarbeit, sondern durch Zinsen eines kleinen Erbes (vgl. ebd., 121). Die Bekanntschaft zwischen ihm und den Beamten resultiert anscheinend aus Dupins bereitwilliger und erfolgreicher Mitarbeit an Kriminalfällen in der Vergangenheit: in „The Murders in the Rue Morgue" erfahren wir, dass ihm der Polizeipräfekt G – ohne Umstände den Zugang zum Tatort erteilt (vgl. ebd., 133). Das Verhältnis zu den Kollegen bei der örtlichen Polizei ist stets von seinem Überlegenheitsgefühl geprägt, das teilweise in Spott übergeht: die seiner Meinung nach unangemessenen Methoden der Polizei vergleicht er beispielsweise mit der Literaturfigur Monsieur Jourdain, die einen Schlafrock verlangt, um die Musik besser hören zu können (vgl. ebd., 132).

Während sich in Dupins Kopf analytische Denkvorgänge abspielen, verändert sich sein Wesen: er ist in diesen Momenten kalt und ausdruckslos und die Tonhöhe seiner Stimme macht einen Sprung aufwärts, was in dem Erzähler die Vorstellung eines doppelten Dupins - „*the creative and the resolvent*" (ebda) – erweckt, woraufhin dieser feststellt, dass die Veränderung seines Wesens in dem Zustand des „*auflösenden*" Dupins wohl das Resultat einer fast krankhaft enthusiastischen Intelligenz sein müsse.

Auf das von Kayman angesprochene hohe intellektuelle Interesse (s. o.) verweist sein Freund mit der Bemerkung: *„I was astonished [...] at the vast extent of his reading"* (ebd., 122). Aber Dupin ist nicht nur überdurchschnittlich intellektuell, sondern ein ausgesprochener Exzentriker: *„It was a freak of fancy in my friend [...] to be enamoured of the night for her own sake; and into this bizarrerie, as into all his others, I quietly fell."* (ebda) Dabei wird seine exzentrische Persönlichkeit vom Erzähler als belebend und phantastisch empfunden. (ebd., 121 f)

Etwas Befremdliches hingegen hat Dupins Nationalität an sich, berücksichtigt man den historischen Kontext. So stellt Bloom fest: *„to an American this [his being French], in the nineteenth century, is in a sense exoticism"* (Bloom 1988, 20). Auch sein fast asozialer Lebensstil, den er mit dem Erzähler gemeinsam pflegt, ist exotisch. Die beiden Protagonisten schotten sich völlig von ihren Mitmenschen ab, sind nachtaktiv und erlauben keine Besucher. (vgl. Poe 1994, 122) *„Had the routine of our life at this place been known to the world, we should have been regarded as madmen."* (ebda)

In einigen Punkten ähneln sich die Figurendarstellungen von Dupin und Holmes. Auch Holmes' Persönlichkeit wird uns von seinem Gefährten vermittelt, auch dieser konstruiert das Bild eines analytischen Genies. Jedoch beschränkt sich Doyle größtenteils auf den Handlungsablauf, um diesen Effekt zu erzielen. Die Handlung ist immer auf Holmes Seite, bestätigt immer seine unglaublichen Fähigkeiten. Sei es, dass er, ohne auch nur ein Wort mit Watson gewechselt zu haben, errät, dass dieser gerade aus Afghanistan kommt (vgl. Doyle 2004, 6), oder anhand der wenigen Spuren am ersten Tatort verblüffend detailreiche Aussagen über Täter und Tathergang machen kann (vgl. ebd., 26), die sich später als Fakten bestätigen. Doyle hat die Feder schließlich in der Hand und kann die Handlung immer so steuern, dass sie Holmes übermenschlich intelligent erscheinen lässt. Watson hält sich mit Hochachtungsbekundungen im Vergleich zu Dupins Freund eher zurück, seine empörte Haltung Holmes gegenüber („*I was still annoyed at his bumptious style of conversation*", ebd., 17) weicht nur nach und nach dem Respekt: „*I confess that I was considerably startled by this fresh proof of the practical nature of my companion's theories.*" (ebd., 18).

Wie auch Dupin repräsentiert Holmes den Intellekt, jedoch differenziert Doyle bei Holmes den Wissensbegriff: Philosophie oder Astronomie interessieren Holmes nicht, dementsprechend besitzt er auf diesen Gebieten kaum Wissen. In den Bereichen, die seiner Detektivarbeit wichtig erscheinen, verfügt er hingegen über ein enzyklopädisches Wissen (vgl. ebd., 12 f). Auch Holmes lebt trotz seines Intellekts wie Dupin in eher bescheidenen finanziellen Verhältnissen: seine Unterkunft kann er ohne Mitbewohner nicht finanzieren (vgl. ebd., 4). Genau wie Dupin scheint er außerhalb des detektivischen Bereichs keine sozialen Beziehungen zu pflegen außer zum Erzähler.

Doch während uns Poe durch seinen anonymen Erzähler von einem aufregenden, voller lebhafter Phantasie sprudelnden Genie erzählt, kommt das Genie Holmes durch Watson eher kaltblütig daher: „*Holmes is a little too scientific for my tastes – it approaches to cold-bloodedness*" (ebd., 5), "'*This fellow may be very clever,*' I said to myself, 'but he is certainly very conceited.*" (ebd., 17) Trotzdem wirkt Holmes etwas nahbarer als Dupin. Er ist als mitten in London lebender Engländer weniger befremdlich als der Franzose: "*the physical world in which Holmes operates is basically that of the natural audience [...] and many streets are those the readers would walk through to catch their trains.*" (Knight 1980, 94) Er hat teil am sozialen Leben und weist somit weniger asoziale Tendenzen auf als Dupin: Er empfängt ständig Besucher in seiner Wohnung (vgl. Doyle 2004, 13), ist in der Regel tagaktiv, arbeitet im Labor (vgl. ebd., 10) und geht ins Konzert (vgl. ebd., 32). Dafür stattet Doyle seinen Holmes mit einer weiteren sonderbaren Eigenschaft aus: die merkwürdige Gewohnheit, einer auf seinen Knien liegenden Violine seltsame, atonale Klänge zu entlocken (vgl. ebd., 13).

Holmes Beziehung zu einigen Beamten der Berufspolizei von Scotland Yard ist hingegen wieder mit der des Dupin zu vergleichen, jedoch wird diese hier etwas klarer geschildert. Holmes scheint in seiner Funktion als Amateur-Detektiv etwas etablierter als Dupin zu sein. „*'I'm a consulting detective*'" (ebd., 15), erklärt er Watson. Wenn Staats- oder Privatdetektive sich nicht mehr zu helfen wüssten, konsultierten sie ihn. Mit dieser Tätigkeit verdient Holmes im Gegensatz zu Dupin sein täglich' Brot (vgl. ebda). Wie Dupin fühlt er sich ihnen so überlegen, dass er sich stets über sie lustig macht. Polizist Gregson hält er zwar für „*'the smartest of the Scotland Yarders*'", sich selbst jedoch für schlauer („*'He knows that I am his superior*'") und übernimmt den Mordfall in der Gewissheit, später über die Scotland-Yard-Polizisten lachen zu können: „*'I shall work it out on my hook. I may have a laugh at them, if I have nothing else.*'" (ebd., 19 f)

Ein zwiespältiges Wesen wie Dupin scheint auch Holmes zu sein. Watson bemerkt, dass sein Mitbewohner mal von Arbeitswut, mal von völliger Trägheit überfallen wird:

> „Nothing could exceed his energy when the working fit was upon him; but now and again a reaction would seize him, and for days on end he would lie upon the sofa in the sitting-room, hardly uttering a word or moving a muscle from morning to night. On these occasions I have noticed such a dreamy, vacant expression in his eyes that I might have suspected him of being addicted to the use of some narcotic" (ebd., 10) [54]

---

[54] In *The Sign of Four* macht Watson die Entdeckung, dass Holmes zu diesen Zeiten tatsächlich unter dem Einfluss von Kokain steht (vgl. Cranny-Francis 1988, 93). Interessanterweise findet sich die Anwendung von Rauschgift nicht bei Dupin, sondern bei Poe selbst wieder. „*Es mag sein, daß [sic] Doyle hier direkt aus der Persönlichkeit des amerikanischen Dichters [...] geschöpft hat.*" (Depken 1977, 88)

Dupin und Holmes scheinen im Ansatz sehr ähnliche Charakterzüge zu besitzen, so dass man annehmen kann, dass Doyle Dupin durchaus als Vorlage für seinen Holmes benutzt, dann aber noch Feinheiten variiert und hinzugefügt hat. Im Gegensatz zu Poe gab er seiner Detektivfigur auch mit einem auffälligen, entschlossen wirkendem Aussehen eine äußere Erscheinung: eine große, hagere Gestalt mit lebhaftem und durchdringendem Blick, einer spitzen Nase und einem scharfkantig vorstehendem Kinn (vgl. ebda).

Methode

Das zentrale Charakteristikum der Methode Dupins ist *„a peculiar analytic ability"* (Poe 1994, 122), wie sein namenloser Freund sie nennt. Die erste Kostprobe seiner analytischen Begabung, die Dupin seinem Freund bei einem Spaziergang demonstriert, ist verblüffend. Er besitzt scheinbar die Gabe, Gedanken zu lesen. Doch genauer betrachtet stecken hinter dem analytischen Kunststück keine übermenschlichen Fähigkeiten, sondern neben bemerkenswert analytischen Schlussprozessen zwei grundlegende Kriterien als Basis für diese Schlussfolgerungen: *„Dupin's knowledge of the narrator's recent experience and close observation of his gestures and movements."* (Knight 1980, 42) Dupin hat das Verhalten seines Begleiters, jeden Gesichtsausdruck, jede Kopfbewegung genauestens beobachtet. Ebenso besitzt er das Wissen über bestimmte Erfahrungen, die der Erzähler gemacht hat, nämlich durch ein kürzlich stattgefundenes gemeinsames Gespräch sowie einen Zeitungsartikel, den der Erzähler Dupins Wissen nach gelesen haben muss. (vgl. Poe 1994, 125 f) Er kombiniert seine scharfen Beobachtungen des Begleiters mit dem Wissen über ihn und gelangt über kognitive Schlussprozesse zu dem exakten Gedanken, der dem Begleiter soeben durch den Kopf gegangen ist. Oft reicht Dupins Wissen bis in alltagsfernste Spezialgebiete hinein, Bloom spricht von einem *„'encyclopaedic' mind"*: *„[His] ability in one specific area looks as if it* *encompasses all areas of knowledge.*" (Bloom 1988, 21) Anhand der Beschaffenheit eines am Tatort gefundenen Haarbandes schließt Dupin beispielsweise darauf, dass es sich bei dem Besitzer dieses Bandes um einen Matrosen eines Malteser Schiffes handelt, weil Dupin das spezielle Wissen über Malteser-Seeleute besitzt (vgl. Poe 1994, 147). Weiterhin gelangt Dupin zur Lösung des Falls einerseits durch sein Wissen über anatomische Besonderheiten von Orang-Utans, das er sich über die Literatur des Zoologen Cuvier angelesen hat (vgl. ebd., 146), und andererseits über wichtige Beobachtungen am Tatort, die der Polizei entgangen sind: er entdeckt beispielsweise einen scheinbar heilen Nagel am Fensterrahmen, der tatsächlich zerbrochen ist, und somit den Fluchtweg des Täters. (vgl. ebd., 140).

Auch Holmes Begabung ist es, Schlussfolgerung in Kombination mit aufmerksamen Beobachtungen und weit überdurchschnittlichem Wissen durchzuführen. „*'Yes, I have a turn both for observation and for deduction'*"(Doyle 2004, 15), erklärt er seinem Freund Watson. Er beobachtet einen Passanten auf der Straße durch das Fenster und erkennt anhand eines Tatoos auf der Hand und seiner Haltung, dass er Seargent bei der Marine war und liegt mit dieser Vermutung richtig. (vgl. ebd., 17 f) Wie Dupin in „The Murders in the Rue Morgue" macht Holmes am Tatort seines Falls in *A Study in Scarlet* aufgrund genauster Überprüfungen – „*with the most minute exactness*", bemerkt Watson (ebd., 25) – Entdeckungen, die Scotland Yard entgangen sind. Genauso wie Dupin verfügt er über enzyklopädisches Wissen, im Gegensatz zu diesem jedoch ausschließlich auf den Gebieten, die ihm für seine Arbeit wichtig erscheinen: „*'He said that he would acquire no knowledge which did not bear upon his object'*" (ebd., 12). Sogar elementarstes Allgemeinwissen interessiert ihn nicht. So hält er die Lehre des Kopernikus für „*lumber*", während er aber über ein für seine Detektivarbeit relevantes Wissen verfügt (Kriminalstatistik, Chemie, britisches Recht etc.), das tief greifender und umfassender nicht sein könnte (vgl. ebd., 11 ff). Und hinter dieser Wissensdifferenzierung steckt Systematik: „*'for every addition of knowledge you forget something that you knew before. It is of the highest importance, therefore, not to have useless facts elbowing out the useful ones.'*" (ebda), erklärt Holmes. Die wichtigste Besonderheit, die den Methoden Dupins' und Holmes' gemeinsam ist, besteht also in einer besonderen analytischen Denkweise, mit der Voraussetzung einer scharfsinnigen Beobachtungsgabe und der Abfragemöglichkeit von erstaunlich tief gehendem und breit angelegtem Wissen.

Dupin wird bezüglich seiner Methode häufig als *armchair detective* bezeichnet, was nur teilweise zutrifft, wie auch Knight feststellt: „[…] *he can also be a man of action. [...] his inquiries in the Rue Morgue are detailed and much more accurate than those of the police. Dupin is not an armchair detective [...]* " (Knight 1980, 42) Dennoch kann man den *armchair detective* in Dupin nicht ganz leugnen. Solange es angebracht scheint, analysiert er den Fall sehr wohl aus der Distanz heraus. Jahshan zitiert diesbezüglich Werner: *"Werner describes Dupin arriving 'at a clearer understanding of the situation by 'removing' himself from the crime scene and focusing on newspaper accounts of the crime"* (Jahshan 2002, 84) Beispielsweise gelangt Dupin durch die in einem Zeitungsartikel wiedergegebenen Zeugenaussagen über die Sprache des Täters (vgl. Poe 1994, 126 ff) zu dem Schluss, dass der Täter keine menschliche Sprache spricht, ergo kein Mensch ist (vgl. ebd., 136 ff). Gerade die Indirektheit und die Zusammengefasstheit der Zeugenaussagen im Zeitungsartikel legen diesen Schluss offen.

Bei Holmes verhält es sich ähnlich. Ohne zu zögern sucht er den Ort des Geschehens (vgl. Doyle 2004, 20 f) auf und befragt auch selbst den Zeugen, der als erstes dort war (vgl. ebd., 29 f), denn „*It is a capital mistake to theorise before you have all the evidence.*'", so Holmes (ebd., 20). *Armchair detective* ist er im späteren Verlauf der Handlung, als er sich den Ablauf weiterer

Ermittlungen zum Mordfall von seinen Freunden Lestrade und Gregson vom Scotland Yard nur berichten lässt. Ihre falschen Schlüsse belächelt er nur und zieht stillschweigend seine eigenen aus den Berichten: „*'The last link,'*" triumphiert er schließlich, „*'My case is complete'*" (ebd., 49). Ein weiteres, gemeinsames Charakteristikum der Methoden unserer Detektive sind also zwei Vorgehensweisen, einmal als *armchair detective*, wenn sie in Abwesenheit von Ermittlungen Zusammenhänge aufdecken, und einmal als „*men of action*", wenn sie eigene Ermittlungen durchführen.

Weiterhin gehört es zur Methode Dupins, sich nicht durch das beirren zu lassen, was die Polizei bereits als Unmöglichkeit erwiesen haben will (beispielsweise die anscheinend vernagelten Fenster als Fluchtweg), wodurch sich die Beamten selbst in Verwirrung bringen, so dass sie den Weg zur Lösung nicht finden. Dupin bemerkt: „*'They have fallen into the gross but common error of confounding the unusual with the abstruse.'*" (Poe 1994, 135). Daher sucht er mit dem Erzähler selbst den Tatort auf, um sich eine eigene Meinung zu verschaffen: „*'let us enter into some examinations for ourselves, before we make up an opinion'*" (ebd., 133). Während also die Polizei von allen scheinbaren *Unmöglichkeiten* irregeleitet den Fall für durch und durch *abstrus* hält, wird Dupin von der vernünftigen Annahme geleitet, dass es eine alles entscheidende *Möglichkeit* geben muss: Dupin eliminiert alle tatsächlichen Unmöglichkeiten und kommt zu dem Schluss, dass der Täter durch ein Hinterfenster entkommen sein *muss*. „*'It is only left for us to prove that these apparent ,impossibilities' are, in reality, not such.'*" (ebd., 138). Sayers spricht hier von einem der „*großen Aphorismen der wissenschaftlichen Detektivarbeit*", das in dieser Geschichte „*zum ersten Male verkündet*" (Sayers 1977, 153) werde. Depken stellt zudem fest, dass die Fokussierung auf Möglichkeiten anstatt auf alle scheinbaren Unmöglichkeiten nicht nur typisch für Dupins', sondern auch Holmes' Methode ist (vgl. Depken 1977, 82). In *A Study In Scarlet* findet sich hierzu folgende Erklärung Holmes: „*'Hence things which have perplexed you and made the case more obscure have served to enlighten me and to strengthen my conclusions. It is a mistake to confound strangeness with mystery.*'" (Doyle 2004, 51) Dieser letztere Satz liest sich zudem wie eine direkte Referenz an Dupin und seiner Bemerkung über „*'the gross but common error of confounding the unusual with the abstruse.*'" (s.o.)

Beziehung zwischen Erzähler und Detektiv

Auf den ersten Blick scheint Doyle die Beziehung der beiden Protagonisten in „The Murders in the Rue Morgue" auf die Figuren des Holmes und des Watson übertragen zu haben. Der Zufall lässt jeweils beide aufeinander treffen: Dupin und der Erzähler treffen sich erstmalig in einer Bücherei, *„where the accident of our both being in search of the same very rare and very remarkable volume, brought us into closer communion. "*, wobei nicht ausschließlich der Zufall sie in dieselbe Bücherei geführt hat, sondern offensichtlich auch gemeinsame intellektuelle Interessen (vgl. Poe 1994, 121). Watson lernt Holmes durch einen gemeinsamen Bekannten kennen, den Watson nach Jahren zufällig trifft (vgl. Doyle 2004, 4). Sowohl Dupin und der Erzähler als auch Holmes und Watson beziehen kurz nach dem ersten Treffen eine gemeinsame Wohnung. Soweit scheinen die Beziehungen oberflächlich einen ähnlichen Charakter zu haben. Während jedoch Holmes und Watson ausschließlich aus finanziellen Gründen (vgl. ebda) zusammen ziehen, führen in der Dupin-Geschichte gemeinsame Interessen zunächst zu weiteren Treffen, bis der Erzähler aus dem Interesse an Dupins Gesellschaft heraus, den Wunsch äußert, mit ihm zusammen zu ziehen: *„I felt that the society of such a man would be to me a treasure beyond price; and this feeling I frankly confided to him. It was at length arranged that we should live together"* (Poe 1994, 122). Ihre Beziehung ist von Anfang an gekennzeichnet durch Gemeinsamkeit, Aufrichtigkeit und Verbundenheit. Der Erzähler hat ein großes Interesse an Dupins Person, das er aufrichtig bekundet. Dupin gibt sich aufgeschlossen, indem er von sich und seiner Familie erzählt. (vgl. ebd., 121) Der Erzähler beschreibt, wie er von Dupins Phantasie regelrecht angesteckt wird (*„I felt my soul enkindled within me by the wild fervour, and the vivid freshness of his imagination.*", ebd., 121 f) und allmählich und ohne Rückhalt all seine täglichen Gewohnheiten teilt: *"and into this bizarrerie, as into* *all his others, I quietly fell; giving myself up to his wild whims with a perfect abandon.*" (ebd., 122). Der Alltag der beiden wird stets gefüllt mit gemeinsamen Aktivitäten in enger Verbundenheit: "*we then busied our souls in dreams – reading, writing, or conversing [...]. Then we sallied forth into the streets, arm in arm, continuing the topics of the day*" (ebda). Von Beginn an bewundert der Erzähler Dupins Fähigkeiten, zu analysieren. "*I could not help remarking and admiring [...] a peculiar analytic ability in Dupin.*" (ebda)

Zwar hegt Watson genauso wie Dupins Freund ein Interesse an seinem Mitbewohner, das sich von Tag zu Tag steigert: „*As the weeks went by, my interest in him and my curiosity as to his aims in life gradually deepened.*" (Doyle 2004, 10) Jedoch steckt dahinter nicht das Bedürfnis des Nacheiferns wie bei Dupins Kumpanen, sondern das Interesse an dem Andersartigen. Distanz und Verschlossenheit tritt hier an die Stelle von Nähe und Aufgeschlossenheit: "*I was on the point of asking him what that work might be, but something in his manner showed me that the question would be an unwelcome one.*" (ebd., 12) Vergeblich versucht Watson, Holmes Verschwiegenheit zu durchbrechen: „*how often I endeavoured to break through the reticence which he showed on all that concerned him*" (ebd., 11). So erfährt Watson nur mühsam von Holmes Tätigkeit als beratender Detektiv. Anstatt mehr über ihn im direkten Kontakt in Erfahrung zu bringen, sammelt er insgeheim Hinweise und fertigt eine Liste über Holmes Wissensgebiete an, um darüber vergeblich seine Beschäftigung erraten zu können. (ebd., 12) Watsons Annerkennung für seine Arbeit muss sich Holmes hart erkämpfen. Im ersten Gespräch der beiden über Holmes analytischen Verstand reagiert Watson erbost auf dessen Eingebildetheit: „'*I was still annoyed at his bumptious style of conversation. I thought it best to change the topic.*'" (ebd., 17) Und nachdem die beiden den Tatort ihres ersten gemeinsamen Falles besucht haben, wo Holmes seine Fähigkeiten zum wiederholten Mal unter Beweis stellen konnte, gibt sich Watson immer noch misstrauisch: „*'You amaze me, Holmes,' said I. ‚Surely you are not as sure as you pretend to be af all those particulars which you gave.'*" (ebd., 27). Erst am Ende der Handlung von *A Study In Scarlet* drückt Watson seinen Respekt für den Detektiv aus: „*'Your merits should be publicly recognized. [...] I have all the facts in my journal, and the public shall know them.*'" (ebd., 105 f).

Erzählperspektive

Es bedarf keiner genaueren Betrachtung der vorliegenden Texte, um festzustellen, dass sich Doyle erzählperspektivisch an Poe orientiert: In beiden Fällen handelt es sich um Ich-Erzählungen nach Stanzel (vgl. Genette 1998, 133) mit autodiegetischen Erzählinstanzen (vgl. ebd., 175 ff) und interner Fokalisierung nach Genette (ebd., 134 ff). Darüber hinaus zählen beide Werke zu der *„besonderen Gattung der Zuschauererzählungen"* (Depken 1977, 77), indem der Ich-Erzähler nicht der Held selbst ist, sondern ein interessierter Zuschauer bzw. Freund. Bei Poe ist es der namenlose Freund, bei Doyle Dr. Watson. Dieses Erzählprinzip wurde nach Poe nicht nur von Doyle, sondern auch von anderen Autoren der Detektivliteratur angewendet, was nicht verwunderlich ist, *„denn es ist offensichtlich sehr praktisch für den Autor"* (Sayers 1977, 148). Es bietet einige Vorteile: Wie schon Becker (vgl. Becker 1975, 69), Depken (vgl. Depken 1977, 77) und Sayers (vgl. Sayers 1977, 148 f) feststellen, besteht einer der Vorteile darin, dass die genauen Beobachtungen und Gedanken des Helden verschleiert werden. Die Beschreibungen des Erzählers der Dupin-Geschichte halten uns den Raum, in dem die Tat begangen wurde, nur ungenau vor Augen: *„I saw nothing beyond what had been stated in the Gazette des Tribunaux"* (Poe 1994, 134), sonst beobachtet er lediglich, *dass* Dupin Beobachtungen durchführt, jedoch nicht *welche*: *„Dupin, meanwhile, examining [...] the house, with a minuteness of attention for which I could see no possible object."* (ebda). Tatsachen wie die des zerbrochenen Nagels am Fensterrahmen bleiben uns auf diese Weise zunächst verschwiegen. Dieses Prinzip der Erzählung findet sich in *A Study In Scarlet* wieder. Bei den Ermittlungen am ersten Tatort kann Watson nur beobachten, *dass* Holmes eine Reihe von Beobachtungen durchführt: *„For twenty minutes or more he continued his researches, measuring with the most exact care the distance between marks which were entirely invisible to me"* (Doyle 2004, 25), *welche Entdeckungen* der Detektiv dabei macht, erfahren wir erst später. Die Verschleierung der Gedanken- und Erlebniswelt des Helden schließt Fair Play (vgl. Sayers 1977, 172) aus, bietet die Möglichkeit für Red Herrings (vgl. Becker 1975, 69) und kommt dem Spannungsaufbau erheblich zugute, da der Leser selbst nur Vermutungen über den Tathergang anstellen kann (vgl. Depken 1977, 77). Gleichermaßen machen sie, sobald der Detektiv seine Erkenntnisse äußert, *„die Brillanz der pseudologischen Deduktion aus. Der Roman wird dem Beweis angepasst."* (Becker 1975, 69)

Als einen weiteren und nicht minder wichtigen Vorteil bietet der als Erzähler eingesetzte und mit durchschnittlicher Intelligenz ausgestattete Begleiter des Helden die Möglichkeit der Identifikation (vgl. Knight 1980, 42). Der Leser wird nicht gezwungen, sich in den mit abnormalen Geisteskräften ausgestatteten Helden (Dupin oder Holmes) hineinzuversetzen (vgl. Depken, 1977, 78).

Fazit

Die Analyse macht deutlich, dass sich Doyle bei der Konstruktion seiner Detektivfigur Sherlock Holmes tatsächlich an Poes C. Auguste Dupin orientierte: Der Aspekt der detektivischen Methode und der Erzählperspektive macht die Imitation evident. Dahingegen zeigen die Darstellungen der beiden Persönlichkeiten in einigen Punkten und die Beziehungen zu ihren Gefährten ganz besonders, dass Holmes kein durchgängiges Imitat von Dupin ist.

Sherlock Holmes darf somit Eigenständigkeiten zugesprochen, jedoch nicht ganz ohne Rückbesinnung auf Poes Detektivfigur Dupin betrachtet werden.

Der Umfang dieser Arbeit erlaubte eigentlich nicht viel mehr, als das Thema „C. Auguste Dupin und Sherlock Holmes im Vergleich" nur anzuschneiden. Die beiden Detektivfiguren respektive die entsprechenden Werke könnten noch viel genauer miteinander verglichen werden, um die obige These zu untermauern oder zu entkräften, sei es qualitativ durch die Einbeziehung weiterer Aspekte (z. B. formale) und/oder quantitativ (Untersuchung anhand weiterer Dupin- und Holmes-Stories).

Literaturverzeichnis

Becker, Jens-Peter, *Sherlock Holmes & Co. Essays zur englischen und amerikanischen Detektivliteratur* (München, 1975).

Bloom, Clive, "Capitalising on Poe's Detective: the Dollars and Sense of Nineteenth-Century Detective Fiction", in: *Nighteenth-Century Suspense. From Poe to Conan Doyle*, hg. Clive Bloom et. al. (London, 1988), 14 – 25.

Cranny-Francis, Anne, "Arthur Conan Doyle's The Parasite: the Case of the Anguished Author", in: *Nineteenth-Century Suspense. From Poe to Conan Doyle*, hg. Clive Bloom et. al. (London, 1988), 93 – 106.

Depken, Friedrich, „Sherlock Holmes, Raffles und ihre Vorbilder", in: *Der Detektiverzählung auf der Spur. Essays zur Form und Wertung der englischen Detektivliteratur*, hg. Jens Peter Becker/Paul Gerhard Buchloch (Darmstadt, 1977), 67 – 102.

Doyle, Arthur Conan, *Memories and Adventures* (London, 1944).

Doyle, Sir Arthur Conan, *A Study in Scarlet & The Sign of the Four*, Wordsworth Classics (Ware, 2004).

Genette, Gérard, *Die Erzählung* (München, 1998).

Jahshan, Paul: „The Deferred Voice in 'The Murders in the Rue Morgue'", in: *The Edgar Allan Poe Review*, Volume III, Number 2 (Reading, 2002), 78 – 91.

Kayman, Martin A., „The short story from Poe to Chesterton", in: *The Cambridge Companion to Crime Fiction*, hg. Martin Priestman (Cambridge, 2003), 41 – 58.

Knight, Steven, *Form and Ideology in Crime Fiction* (London, 1980).

Matthews, Brander, „Edgar Allan Poe und die Detektivgeschichte“, in: *Der Detektiverzählung auf der Spur. Essays zur Form und Wertung der englischen Detektivliteratur*, hg. Jens Peter Becker/Paul Gerhard Buchloch (Darmstadt, 1977), 41 – 57.

Poe, Edgar Allan, *Selected Tales*, Penguin Popular Classics (London, 1994).

Sayers, Dorothy L., "Einleitung zu 'Great Short Stories of Detection, Mystery and Horror'", in: *Der Detektiverzählung auf der Spur. Essays zur Form und Wertung der englischen Detektivliteratur*, hg. Jens Peter Becker/Paul Gerhard Buchloch (Darmstadt, 1977), 142 – 190.

Einzelpublikationen

Eva Deinzer (2009): Poe's Tales of Ratiocination - A Closer Look

ISBN: 978-3-656-27270-0

Bernhard Kehler (2009): Geheimnis und Detektion. Edgar Allen Poes Erzählungen "The Murders in the Rue Morgue" und "The Purloined Letter" als Vorbild für ein neues Genre

ISBN: 978-3-640-69240-8

Ines Sundermann (2007): "You remind me of Edgar Allan Poe's Dupin". C. Auguste Dupin und Sherlock Holmes im Vergleich

ISBN: 978-3-640-24642-7